Memoirs of David Palmer

Memoirs of David Palmer

Published by Wheatmark®
610 East Delano Street, Suite 104
Tucson, Arizona 85705 U.S.A.
www.wheatmark.com

International Standard Book Number: 978-1-60494-258-3
Library of Congress Control Number: 2009922594

To contact the author, email Palmer4343@aol.com

Foreword

by C.R. Gibbs, world respected historian of the African Diaspora.

Sir Arthur Conan Doyle once remarked that "no British autobiography has ever been frank and consequently no British autobiography has ever been good." Comes now confidently David Palmer, an Americanized Brit, who has penned a lucid, perceptive, deeply insightful memoir that certainly refutes Doyle's observation.

Born a shopkeeper's son on the eve of the Second World War in the village of Aldbourne, threescore and ten miles outside London, Palmer grows up an introspective, bookish lad who early chafed at the restrictions of the English class system. As evacuees arrive in the countryside to escape the bombing of London, his comfortable, insular world broadens as he meets, among many others, the son and daughter of a "Bermudan father and an English mother." He discovers that despite a difference in skin tone, their brains and humanity shine through the opaque glass of local prejudice. He begins to perceive the interconnectedness of discrimination between classes and between races.

Palmer conducts the reader through the profound social, political, and cultural changes that affect his postwar country. His military service further stokes his innate wanderlust. He relocates to the U.S in the mid-1960s and ultimately settles in Washington, D.C. where his liberal attitudes and commitment to equality made him an eager member of several groups fighting injustice and discrimination. A trip to the South with an African immigrant reminds him how high the walls of bigotry are that he is trying to demolish. He is a parade official at the 1963 March on Washington. He also throws himself into labor organizing, falls in love with and marries a Haitian woman, and starts a family while also working as a butcher for a major local supermarket chain. As the head of a growing interracial family at a time when America was slow to accept such unions, Palmer meanwhile does his best to maintain his activist connections.

Palmer's cogent insights on American society during the tumultuous 1960s and 1970s, from his vantage point in the nation's capital, are priceless. He is often an eyewitness to pivotal events in the city at this time and his book provides a brief, valuable history of the District of Columbia in the final decades of the twentieth century.

He delivers his comments with a certain measure of scholarly detachment. But his words speak with a particular power, poignancy, and relevance. His unique gaze provides a priceless portrait of a man, a nation, and a city.

Prologue

These are the memoirs of David Palmer, who was born on September 20, 1936, in the Village of Aldbourne, Wiltshire, England. The Village of Aldbourne is seventy miles west of London, a long distance in the 1930s. The writer does not make any claim to fame or great importance. These are merely the observations of one man who is entering his seventieth year and has lived in two countries and observed many important events.

Chapter I

My father, Alfred Palmer, and mother, Gertrude Palmer, had four children. The first three children were two years apart; six years later, I was the last child born—my mother was in her mid-forties at my birth. The reader can draw his own conclusions from that fact. My parents owned a bakery and grocery store and drapery business in the small town of Aldbourne. They were Wesleyan Methodists and in that society were classified as Chapel. Chapel meant not the Church of England, which controlled the country and the community at that particular time. The Church of England dated back to when Henry VIII broke off from the Catholic Church and formed the official church of the country. Basically, anyone non-Church of England was second-class, with no voting rights, until the 1800s. This included Catholics and all Protestants who did not belong to the Church of England. The remnants of this status lingered until early twentieth-century England. As children, we had to attend morning Chapel service and Sunday school in the afternoon each and every Sunday, without fail. This was a major factor in the development of my thinking and understanding of Christianity. For Wesleyans, rules were not as strict as for our counterparts, Primitive Methodists. My father drank a bottle of Stout every evening, and a bottle of port was consumed at Christmas.

The information that follows will help the reader to understand the social structure of society.

The Palmer family, at that time, would have been classified as lower middle-class, based on their status as businesspeople. However, as Chapel people who spoke the Wiltshire accent, we were down-classified, as English society was judged by accent. The so-called posh accent of the upper class represented people who had attended so-called public or private schools. The average Wiltshire resident spoke with a country brogue, some more pronounced than others, and my father was part of that category.

The village of Aldbourne was divided between the upper class and the rest of the community. This secondary community consisted of the standard laborer class and my family's group, which was divided again by Chapel and Church of England. The upper classes maintained control of the community and ensured that their status remained secure. It is interesting to note that while visiting Aldbourne seventy years later, the street heading West still has no housing development and continues to be controlled by the upper-class families. It should be understood that the lower and middle-class families in many ways encouraged the status quo in the thirties and going into World War II. I know of many instances where shopkeepers and their customers stood aside to let an upper-class person be served first. Thankfully, my parents never allowed this to happen in our store.

Employment in Aldbourne, prior to World War II, consisted mostly of farming; construction work in Swindon, the local industrial town; and the horse racing stables in the center of the village. The large stables provided employment for local men and many from outside the neighboring area who came into the village. The owner was Major Powell who, like all persons with upper-class status, retained his military title. It should be noted that Major Powell had a son the same age as myself; however, at no time did we ever play with one another, nor did he attend the local school.

This was the Aldbourne that entered World War II, the time of my first memories. In 1939, at three years of age, almost four, I clearly remember continually crying when I was forced to try on my gas mask. As the war moved on, we had less and less use for the gas mask, much to my relief.

The first thing you would note in the structure of the village was that all the young men ages eighteen to thirty-five were leaving to join the military and new factories. Those who remained worked on farms and were exempted from conscription.

The stables closed and became a temporary housing accommodation for military forces. It was so cold in those stables that one young soldier used to come to my father's bakery and sleep overnight, because it was warm. By the time the United States military came into the war, the village had become a home to the Hundred and First Airborne Easy Company, which was featured in the Stephen Ambrose book *Band of Brothers*.

By the time I was five, I had started to realize how the war was impacting the world around me. First and foremost was the fact that no lights could be shown at night; thick curtains covered the windows. Food rationing was in effect, and everyone had a ration book. Needless to say, this had a great impact on our family business, on the amount of food we could sell and where we would get it. My father delivered bread in the surrounding areas and was granted a limited amount of petrol for that purpose. Living in a little village was in no way comparable to living in London and other big cities. We did not experience the bombing, but could hear it in the background. The other great change was the arrival of many evacuees from London; the house next door to ours was occupied by a complete London family. However, the greatest number came as individuals or in pairs staying with other families.

Two of the evacuees had a great impact on me at that time, and much later in my life. They were the son and daughter of a Bermudan father and an English mother. The couple who took them in was an established village family, and active members of the Primitive Methodist church. The first thing that came to our attention was that they were both very brainy and excelled in the school system, as well as the church Sunday school. There had always been a strong rivalry between the two Methodist Sunday schools, who competed with other Methodist churches for awards on biblical knowledge. Their school won, and, I actually heard some people say how unfair it was to bring in those brainy colored people. They have remained my friends since that time, and we stay in close contact from across the Atlantic Ocean.

Children played games in the village, and the oldest games were cops and robbers and cowboys and Indians, which was adjusted to English and Germans. Needless to say, the Germans always ended up the losers in our minds. Parents and all elders continued to talk about life before the war. We had no idea what this other world was like as all we knew were the shortages, soldiers all around us, and planes galore flying overhead. There were two major airbases three miles of each side of the village. Day in and day out they were flying in great formations of ten or more, going either to bomb or, as D-Day came close, preparing for that great moment. We would watch them go over, and soon hundreds of parachutists would descend in the air. This would happen day in and day out and became part of our daily lives. In 1943, as I was at the age of understanding some things about the war that was being fought, my father explained it to me, and continued to compare it to World War I. I knew that we had won a big battle at Alamein, but nothing of the great Russian victories. It was always us and the Americans as we prepared for the great day to come.

My father, on the evening of June 5, 1944, was delivering bread to people who lived near the major airbase named Membury and returned home just after 7 PM. He had been told the whole area would be closed by 7 PM, and told us something big was about to happen. A friend of his stayed on and was kept in, overnight, and released at 6 AM, June 6, 1944. We could hear the planes flying all night, and the vast majority of the American soldiers had left the village. During the day, we heard about the start of the invasion of France and waited for the nine o'clock news that night for the details.

The BBC nine o'clock evening news was the community's major source of information, and our house was a center for neighbors, as my father owned a radio. (It should be noted that in Aldbourne, only 30 percent of the population owned radios, and some had no electricity.) As a six-year-old, I was supposed to be in bed by nine o'clock, but could hear them talking downstairs. Soon, I was allowed to stay up and listen with them, but then it was straight to bed. My mother was the great disciplinarian of the family.

The news gave us, every night, information on Allied advances in France; a little on Italy; and, slowly, more and more reports on the Russian front. The war was slowly coming to an end, at the great expense of the men fighting it. Our next-door neighbor and my father both fought in World War I and remembered the horrors of that time. The neighbor, Frank Jerram, had a son who fought in this war, but security shielded him from any information. No bad news came and the son, Gerald, survived the war.

These memories of World War II are of a young boy three to eight years old and are, therefore, limited in detail. My oldest sister, who was sixteen in 1944, had an American boyfriend—I remember some gifts of candy. One day, he took me up the church tower. He was wounded on D-Day and my sister went to visit him in the hospital. However, that was the end of the relationship as he was shipped back to the USA. Three of her friends married American soldiers, as did many other English girls.

The last year of World War II remains strongly in my memory. We followed the progress of the Allies through Europe in the daily papers. A map was printed showing progress on both the Eastern and Western fronts. I don't know how accurate these maps were, due to security, as I never heard about the Battle of the Bulge until the war was over.

V-E Day came on May 9, 1944, and the British celebrated even though the war in Japan continued. The center of the village held huge celebrations crowned with a gigantic bonfire. One of the community leaders produced some secretly held gasoline, which was poured on the fire to the excitement of all around. I stood there with my father, and soon there was screaming with fear as one of the men fell in the fire as he poured in the gasoline. He was dragged out and survived, but from then on was always known as "the man who fell in the fire on V-E Day."

Chapter II

The first thing I noticed as the war ended was the arrival of many new young men in the village. They were, of course, the very people who had left in 1939 and 1940 to serve in the army and work in war factories. Some were my friends' fathers, who had only seen their families occasionally. One boy, two years younger than I, did not see his father because his father had died in a prisoner of war camp in Burma. The village had a public memorial hall, which was dedicated to those who had died in World War I. Noticeably, the new plaque for World War II is a quarter of the size of its predecessor.

The race horse stables reopened and the village tried to return to normal. Food and clothing rationing continued on after the war. There were still shortages of everything, as England was not self-supporting in food and other products. Manufacturers had concentrated on war supplies, and factories needed to be reprogrammed. It was difficult to imagine that even in 1946 we were still limited to four ounces of

meat per person per week. As children, we were excited to
see our first banana, and ice cream caused the most excitement among children.

I had commenced school in January of 1942, even
though I had turned five on September 20, 1941. A quirk
in the English system prevented my going at that time, as
term had already begun. This, of course, put me behind my
fellow classmates; however, over the years I caught up, with
the exception of three very clever girls. The school, itself was
controlled by the Church of England, and all students in the
village attended. We were required to learn the tenets of the
Church of England, and my second-class status was reem-
phasized as a Methodist. This was the start of my resentment
of the English class system.

My schooling showed me to be a very moderate student,
with the exception of history and geography, at which I excelled. At the age of seven, I was able to find Montevideo on
the map, to the amazement of my teacher, but arithmetic and
penmanship were weak. Probably my strict Methodist and
family background forced me to strive harder. On Sunday I
had to spend my afternoon in Sunday school studying the
Bible according to the standards expounded by my teachers.
After the evacuation, my friends of Bermudan descent returned to their parents, and our Sunday school was awarded
the Scripture prize. My Sunday school teacher was the local
leader of the Labor Party and influenced some of my political thinking. It should be understood that at this young age,
I had not developed any political thinking, and in fact, my

father disliked Labor. However, this man impressed me, and I grew to respect his views in my more formative years.

The Labor Party won the election in 1946 and changed the social structure of the British society. The war and politics curtailed the power of the old elite and the aristocracy. It did not become a level playing field but genuine changes were apparent. Class structure in the village remained, but mostly in the minds of the snobs. Farm employment went down, as tractors and other mechanical equipment were introduced. Many of the workers found employment in the nearby town of Swindon and also entered the construction industry. By 1947 the nuclear age had the country starting its own nuclear research facility fifteen miles from the village. A bus picked up workers, who had once led horses on the farm, to become cleaners at a much higher wage.

In 1946, our teachers at the village school started training us for what was known as the 11 plus exam. This was to be the divider for all children in England. Those who passed would have a chance at an academic school, and the remainder would be left with limited opportunities at the so-called secondary modern school. I passed the exam and was scheduled to enter a grammar school in the nearby town of Marlborough. Students from my village were required to board during the week. A bus picked us up on Monday mornings and returned us on Friday evenings. We were joined in this boardinghouse, named Wye House, by children from other outlying villages. In retrospect, I can see that this was to my advantage. My parents were always too busy with the shop and could not have assisted me with my homework assignments. For six years, I became a part-time citizen of the town of Marlborough.

With the exception of the few brilliant students, we found the work hard, but over the years we adjusted. Though a few dropped out, most of us graduated with good O levels (exams somewhat comparable to SATs). My later birthdate caused me to stay on another year, as I was not sixteen years old during exam time. During that year, I took advanced-level study in history and geography. My academic achievements were rewarded with the school history prize for 1954. As a young boy and teenager, I was interested in sports—mostly football (soccer)—but to my disappointment, I was always unsuccessful. At that time, I thought it was partly because I was shorter than my teammates. However, in later years, I discovered that I had spasticity (inherited from my parents). I did achieve some success in long-distance running and became an active cyclist. It is difficult to believe, at the time of this writing, that I used to cycle up to London every summer to visit my aunt and cousins.

Though a nonparticipant, I followed all sports, mostly cricket and football. My brother-in-law was a great footballer, though never on the professional scale. I attended games, supported the local team, and, whenever possible, attended the local, professional club in Swindon. Television coverage in the area did not start until the 1950s, and professional games were not shown until 1957. I initially viewed television in 1948 while visiting my aunt in London. At that time the Olympics of London were being shown. This was new to all of as there had been no Olympics since 1936 in Berlin. This visit to London included a review of many of the bombed areas and the work being performed to clean up. It should be remembered that I had not experienced any bombing—I only read about it.

In the 1950s, I made a new friend, Nick Monro, who now lived in Aldbourne and stayed with me at Wye House. Nick's middle-class family was more worldly than my puritanical Chapel society. His mother, in 1951, married an up-and-coming BBC star named Johnny Morris. Over the years, this association helped me to become a much more modern young man and deal with the world around me. Nick found amusing my resentment of posh accents and preferences given to the upper classes. His family was close to the group, but never quite accepted it. It was during this period of my life that I devoted much of my time to thinking about my beliefs.

After the Labor Party came into power in 1946, they introduced a national health service, increased taxes on the high income brackets, and generally changed the social structure of England. The Conservative Party regained power in 1952 and tried to reverse some of these trends. However, Britain would never be the same again; the Tories accepted the New Order. Though most of the people around me supported the Conservatives, I moved to the Labor fold.

I was lucky to have a first-rate history teacher named Jim Buckley. He was able to present history without the phony nationalism usually attached to it. First and foremost, we learned that twentieth-century Britain evolved from the Industrial Revolution, which started in the eighteenth century and fully developed in the nineteenth-century. These events made Britain a dominant power in the world and ushered in political changes and real democracy. The Britain of the Middle Ages, with the glories of Agincourt, Henry VIII, and Queen Elizabeth successes against Spain were wonderful to celebrate, but meant little to the twentieth century. The Britain of the nineteenth century was very similar in structure and attitude to the United States of the twentieth century. They were the dominant power with the strongest navy and concerned only with their main rival, France.

I left school to participate full-time in the family-owned business, of course. I had always worked in the shop when I was not attending class, so it was a natural transition. My mother and father retired, my brother took over the bakery, and I worked in the grocery store. It was not so much of a choice, but it was considered natural to the family. However, one change came, which meant conscription into the military. In 1954, I got the traditional letter from Her Majesty's Government requiring me to serve for two years. I realized enough at that time to know that life would be a lot easier in the RAF and to confirm that appointment. I volunteered to go for three years.

I reported to RAF Cardington, where I was instructed on my future in the RAF and given inoculations, uniforms, and the like. This base was interesting as hangars for storing airships left over from World War II remained. After a week, we moved on to the basic training facility at Hednesford, a miserable-looking place north of Birmingham. Of course, it was winter, and there was nothing pleasant about basic training. We marched, trained, and became fit and learnt how to shoot rifles, deal with gas attacks, and train in assault courses. Once again, I was one of the smallest in my group, but I survived. We all passed on and were assigned to our career position. So it was back to Cardington for me, where I was advised that I would be a clerk of equipment accounts, stationed at RAF Larbruch in Germany. We traveled by train to Harwich on the east coast, by a military ship to a port in Holland, and from there by train into Germany. The trip across the North Sea in March was absolutely miserable. I, along with many others, spent the time in the bathroom. Holland was very cold, as was Northern Germany. We were transported from the railroad station to our new base, where I lived for the next two and a half years.

RAF Larbruch was a new base. Considered very modern during those days, it contained small barracks (only twelve to a room) and good hot water showers. We were given a short orientation and were told to report to our respective offices the following morning. My office was known as the equipment provisioning and accounting section, or EPAS. Each clerk was assigned to maintain an inventory of supplies. There were no such things as computers; all record-keeping was handwritten. We sat in this huge room overseen by a senior sergeant who was, in turn, overseen by the officer in charge, a man who occupied an office with a window overlooking the room.

The early experience at both basic training and the new base brought me into contact with young men from various sections of Britain. Many of them had never traveled much farther than their homes. Compared to others I was probably more worldly, having traveled to London and most of Southern England. I befriended people from Manchester, Liverpool, Newcastle, and various communities throughout Britain. There were a surprising number of career airmen from Scotland, and even Southern Ireland, which was officially independent. The most interesting character was a Baptist from County Cork, who somehow thought he needed to convert Catholics to Protestantism. As a clerk, I was classified as part of the administrative wing of the base. This group consisted of accountants, secretaries, cooks, and anyone outside the technical arena. Our wing commander loved to address us in Churchillian tones in honor of his World War II hero.

The base operated two squadrons of Canberra bombers who were prepared to fight the Russians at NATO's calling. This, of course, never happened, and the bombers were used for photographic reconnaissance. We were familiar with the bomb storage areas, but not as familiar with bunker containments. In addition, there was a squadron of the Dutch Air Force with similar purposes. The base was guarded by the Royal Air Force Regiment. We, as clerks, felt sorry for them because they had to parade everywhere, while we were almost considered civilians.

We were located just over the border from Holland, and weekend activities were usually in the towns of Nijmegen, Holland, and Krefeld, Germany. A bus laid over every Saturday morning at 10 AM. I managed to buy a used bicycle, which was essential for traveling to the local railroad station, from where I could go farther, often to Amsterdam, a wonderful city. However, my main activity on leave was travel. I covered much of Europe and managed to visit a lot of Germany, as well as Switzerland, Denmark, Sweden, Norway, Holland, and Belgium. I made all of these visits outside of Germany by hitchhiking and staying in youth hostels.

France did not lend itself to hitchhiking, so that meant special bus excursions to Paris and surrounding areas. This was a valuable experience for me, and I came to appreciate all the people of Europe. This was a Europe recovering from World War II and preparing to enter the new United Europe. Britain was very popular at that time, and I carried a Union Jack on my backpack. This helped me to get many lifts into countries that had been occupied by Germany during the war. In Norway, a driver double-checked to make sure I wasn't a "Tisk," or German. The youth hostel system was well organized and provided cheap and moderate boarding. It was interesting to note that there were more Australians than any other country from outside Europe.

Everyday life on the air base was very limited. We had a cinema, café, and churches. There were no television sets, and newspapers from England arrived a day late. The churches were divided into three groups: Church of England, Roman Catholic, and other Protestants. I, of course, belonged to the other group, along with Presbyterians, Quakers, and Baptists. Our chaplain arranged for us to go on special retreats, which was a relief from life as a clerk.

In 1956, two events occurred that reinforced my moderate left-wing thinking. A group of us helped organize a boycott of the airmen's mess when the air officer commander visited the base. It was a great success, to the embarrassment of our commanding officers, because this had never occurred under their command. That year also exposed Britain and France for their failures in Suez. I was absolutely convinced that this war was a continuation of mistaken colonialism.

At that time, military structure emphasized the class distinctions of Britain. The vast majority of officers came from the upper classes with the so-called "posh accent." Many of my fellow airmen who had grown up in London, Birmingham, or other large cities rather than a rural community had not experienced this class structure. They probably resented it more than I did. In fact, I knew of one soldier who, if he noticed an officer in a bar and out of uniform (he was in civilian clothing), would pour beer all over him. This was a very petty action, but I understood the general resentment. To explain this structure, I will quote from a memo on dining: "Officers dine in the officers' mess, sergeants eat in the sergeants' mess, airmen feed in the airmen's mess." During my three years in the air force, the only officer I was ever friendly with was the chaplain.

I completed my military career in November of 1957, having reached the heights of corporal in charge of the clothing store. After demobilization, I was suited up with clothes for civilian life. Tradition said that I must return to the family business, so David Palmer ran the grocery side, and my brother the bakery. Self-service started to come into Britain in the late fifties, and we joined in with discounts to attempt to defeat the competition. I was not completely satisfied with my lot, but accepted the inevitable.

Britain in the 1950s changed as the years progressed. The postwar shortages disappeared, the Conservative Party came into power and started to become more moderate by the end of the decade. After the Suez fiasco, Prime Minister Eden was eliminated and a more progressive group took charge under Macmillan. I still did not support them but was relieved to see the improvements. In Aldbourne, some of the remnants of class distinction were disappearing, mostly due to the financial reforms instituted under the Labor Party, which curtailed their power. The racing stables disappeared due to drug scandals and my parents built a bungalow on some of the land.

British colonial power was also diminishing, and colonies all over the globe became independent. Many of the old upper-class types were aghast when the Gold Coast became Ghana. By the late 1950s, a growing nonwhite population was moving into Britain from India, Pakistan, Uganda, the West Indies, and other parts of Africa. My contacts with the groups of nonwhites were limited, as they settled mostly in London and the Midlands.

My Methodist affiliation continued, and I worked with my brother in showing films and raising money for missionary work overseas. This was my mother's favorite charity, and also emphasized my interest in the people of the world. However, as the decade came to an end, my religious interests mellowed. My brother was the opposite; he continued as a strong Methodist lay preacher. My life centered more around old school friends in Marlborough and visits to my friend Nick in London. He was attending Chelsea Art School, preparing to become a leading sculptor in Britain. Even in those days, Kings Road Chelsea was a major center for young people. My love life varied with no special interest developing. The only serious girlfriend I'd had was prior to RAF; she sent me a Dear John letter while I was in Germany.

My overseas travels in the late fifties were to the World's Fair in Brussels and summer vacations in Barcelona and San Sebastian in Spain. At that time, Spain was still under the control of Franco and was very close to a Third World country compared to the rest of Europe.

By late 1959, my father became ill with bladder cancer and suffered from dementia. I had become very frustrated with the family business, and my brother wanted to run it as a charity organization. There was no way it could support two breadwinners. However, my father's situation delayed the inevitable. I still wanted to travel to other parts of the world. In the mid-1960s I decided on the United States. I applied for a resident visa, which was granted to me based on my financial status, and at that time almost automatic for Western Europeans.

Chapter III

During the last few months of 1960, I prepared for my departure from England, saying goodbye to friends and family and not realizing when I would ever return. It was a gigantic step, but I knew it was inevitable.

Some observations on the England I was leaving, including its people, social conditions, values, and, of course, politics: Since World War II, the country had become more egalitarian, even in the rural areas. The Conservatives were in power, and some were considering uniting with Europe. Colonies had started to become independent, and the belief that the sun never sets on the British Empire was disappearing. Of course, this kind of thinking was far from unanimous, and right-wing politicians exploited the call to national pride. The BBC and independent television covered the country and indirectly contributed to the breakdown of old values and class restructuring. New comedians made fun of all the old-fashioned standards. *The Goon Show* on the radio started the trend and others soon followed. Religious attendance on Sundays was dropping, and the power of the Church of England declined. Methodists, and even the Roman Catholics, were getting closer to a equal social standing. It must be noted that there was still a continuing fear and resentment of the Catholic Church. The Pope, to some, seemed like a threat, and the Church's World War II performance was remembered by many. England's Jewish population was centered in London, with a scattering in Birmingham and Manchester. My contact had always been very limited, except for a few salespeople who came to the shop and my friend's Jewish girlfriend in London. I was aware that some of the best Labor members of Parliament were of the Jewish faith.

My knowledge of the United States was based on my studies in both history and geography, and very often influenced by Hollywood and the television news. British people still thought highly of President Roosevelt, and Eisenhower was the man who helped us win the war. Now, of course, we were interested in a new leader by the name of Kennedy. This was tempered by the usual anti-Catholic bias in parts of society. One of the few people who my family and Methodist Associates admired was Paul Robeson. We knew nothing of the McCarthy era or how he had been associated with the Communist Party. In fact, we believed it was too many evil Russians who wanted to control the world and not Communists. My religious commitment had eased over the last few years, but I still considered myself a Methodist, with strong feelings toward justice for *all* people. I knew that Christianity was an important part of American society, but knew nothing of its structure.

I was ready to depart, but first needed to clear up the paperwork and get my visa. My appointment was scheduled at the U.S. Embassy in London on the day before Thanksgiving. It is interesting to note that I knew little about the Thanksgiving holiday. I was easily approved after completing a statement that said I was not a communist and did not intend to come to the United States to commit an immoral act. In February of 1961, my brother and sisters took me to Southampton Dock, where I boarded the *Queen Mary* for New York. Needless to say, crossing the Atlantic in February, in an aging liner, was not extremely comfortable. Along with many others, I became seasick for the first two days, but the last three were quite pleasant, and I became acquainted with my fellow passengers. Many wanted to instruct me on what I should and should not do. I'm sorry to say, a few were quite objectionable concerning what they called the "colored," and said that Franklin Roosevelt was the worst president ever. I kept my opinions to myself, and did not get into any serious arguments.

On arriving in New York, I was met by some relatives of an English girlfriend who had made reservations at a hotel and promised to take me on the town. They were very kind, and I was overwhelmed with the sight of New York skyscrapers and, of course, a trip to the top of what was then the tallest building in the world. After a few days, I was running out of money and knew I must move on. I took the Greyhound bus to Baltimore, where a friend of my sister lived. They were very nice but were not looking for a lodger, so I checked into a rooming house in the city. This was operated by an elderly Jewish lady who would be naturally described as a Jewish

Mama. She was firm but kind and was fascinated by my lack of knowledge of Judaism. At Passover, I was invited to their dinner, eating all the special dishes, and was amazed to watch all the men saying their prayers with their hats on.

My first job in America was selling encyclopedias door-do-door. The boss met us all at 4 PM and gave us instructions for the evening. We were driven to a residential area, knocking on doors and working on commission. On my first night I was successful, selling a complete set and receiving a nice commission. However, that was my only commission, and I realized I had to find something else. I applied for work as a salesman in a downtown department store. This job gave me a limited salary and not much satisfaction. I planned to move on.

Baltimore proved to be my first eye-opening experience of the United States and motivated my first interest in the plight of Black America. A few blocks up the street from my lodging was a wonderful library, which I used regularly, and not far from the other side of the street was the YMCA. The library was open to all, but to my dismay to YMCA was segregated. Perhaps I was naïve, but I had grown up believing in the justice of Christianity. All around me was a huge city completely divided on the basis of race. My fellow white workers usually presented a negative attitude concerning anyone at that time classified as colored. Even my sister's friend and her family had a similar attitude and told me that Washington DC was no good as it had too many colored.

I decided to visit Washington DC and, on my day off, true to old patterns, hitchhiked. This proved to slightly embarrassing, as a person who picked me up turned out to be a homosexual and propositioned me at his apartment. Needless to say, I got out of there very quickly and vowed never to try that again. One interesting sideline about the man was that he worked for a Republican congressman. I looked around this new city, decided it was far superior to Baltimore, and planned to move there. On my return to Baltimore, I quit my job in the department store, said goodbye to the landlady, and moved to Washington, where I found a job quite quickly. It should be noted that though my landlady regretted my departure, she thought some of my ideas concerning segregation—which she adhered to in her rooming house—were strange. However, I will always believe that deep down, she admired my position.

My first job in Washington DC was as a desk clerk at the Airways Hotel at National Airport. These two small buildings provided travelers with short stays between flights. There were two employees on each shift. The clerk was white and the porter Black. My Black coworker and I had long, interesting conversations about the society we were living in. The manager soon complained about this friendliness, and even more when I registered a Black minister into the rooms. I was told this was a complete violation of her policy.

For lodgings in Washington, I was directed to a boarding house in the Adams Morgan area. They provided a room, breakfast, and dinner at night, moderately priced by Washington's standards. Of course, it was a "whites only" facility, though I will admit that a few of my fellow renters did not approve. One couple belonged to the Jehovah's Witness faith, and they asked me to come to service. This service ran on for four hours and made very little sense to me. However, I was pleased with the fact that all races were scattered through the church. I spent much of my time, during the first few weeks, being a tourist, seeing all the sites. There were wonderful museums and monuments, and of course, the White House and the Capitol. I met many interesting people during those first few weeks, and some held similar ideas about the structure of the society. Housing was completely segregated, and most restaurants were open to all. The first stirring of the civil rights movement was beginning to have an effect.

Washington DC, in 1961, was a city of seven hundred thousand people, of whom 70 percent were Black, and it was governed by three appointed commissioners. There were no voting rights whatsoever, and for the first time, the Kennedy administration appointed a Black commissioner. The Congress had a District of Columbia Committee, which was in complete control. The majority of the members of the Committee were Southern Democrats, whose commitment was to their home constituency, who had elected them based on their segregationist thinking.

After settling in Washington DC, I did find a few white Americans whose positions were similar to mine. This was a relief, compared to Baltimore, but the overwhelming number was opposed to everything I said. Needless to say, they regularly called me a "nigger lover." I made one good friend who was a Catholic of Lebanese descent and had many interests similar to mine. He invited me to join him in leasing a house with another guy, which was much more economical than the boardinghouse. Soon, we were joined by another friend who was of American Indian descent. In addition, I changed my job and became an apprentice butcher with the Safeway supermarket. This represented a considerable increase in pay and membership in a trade union. I was able to become a stable and productive part of the workforce. I brought a car and saw myself turning into a twentieth-century American.

I worked in several Safeway stores as I started to learn my trade and ended up in a permanent location at Fourteenth and U Streets, Northwest, which turned out to be the cultural center of Black Washington. This was not my choice, but a company decision, which proved invaluable to me and my ideals. At the same time, my Catholic friend had taken me to join a group called the Young Christian Workers at Blessed Sacrament Church in Chevy Chase, Maryland. They met me once; when I announced that I was Protestant, it was goodbye. My friend turned around and took me to St. Paul and Augustine's Catholic Church, at Fifteenth and V Streets, Northwest, where I met Father Gino Baroni. Father Baroni was forming his own group, where both Catholics and Protestants were welcome. Not only was it close to my work, but the group that formed consisted of both Black and white members. I also enrolled in the Dale Carnegie Leadership course after graduation and was voted one of their best students. It was interesting and gave me great insights into American standards. I was now becoming a determined citizen of the United States who wanted to play a part in its future.

As an English immigrant into the United States, I was immediately treated as a first-class citizen. The class distinctions I had experienced were long gone. Class in the United States was not based on accent but on financial status. However, at this time, I chose to attack a system of racism that was far more evil than anything I had ever experienced. My life in England had been a piece of cake compared to that of any American of African descent.

I have already noted that I was not a tall, imposing figure, with great physical strength. However, I did possess a strong will and determination to get my point across. At times, this was making my life very difficult whenever I was in a predominantly white crowd or even in simple conversation. To make my life little easier, while holding to my views, I decided to move with two Black friends from YCW into a house at Fifteenth and R Streets, Northwest, a predominantly Black section of the city. Now I felt secure, away from the more hostile white world.

This was the USA in Washington DC in 1962, a year after leaving England. My original concepts and understandings of the United States were now considerably changed. I knew it was a large country with a population of over two hundred million, but did not know that the concentration was mostly on the East and West Coasts, with pockets like Chicago and New Orleans in between. The Hollywood presentations, which governed the thinking of most Western Europeans, had provided false impressions. Not all Americans were rich. They did not live in large apartment buildings, but mostly in nice individual houses. The majority of white Americans were descended from immigrants from all over Europe. We had thought nineteenth-century America had a population of primarily English and Irish origin, when in fact there were more Germans scattered all over the country than the English. The early twentieth-century Americans were from Italy, Greece, and Central European countries such as Poland. Religion was very strong throughout the United States, and the country was far more puritanical than the Europeans realized. We had grown up during World War II with the saying that the "Yanks are over here and oversexed." By 1962, I realized that it was the Europeans who were oversexed, and that they should be thankful the Yanks were over there in World War II. The other thing I had misunderstood was the U.S. paranoia about communism. I knew nothing of the McCarthy hearings, but soon learned how many human beings had been destroyed. As I stated earlier, I had been along the long admirer of Paul Robeson, who we never thought of as an evil communist, but a great humanitarian.

As regards to the status of Black Americans, I had been completely uninformed. I knew about the situation in Little Rock, Arkansas, but thought this was an isolated incident. The size of the Black population—11 percent of the nation—was new to me. In fact, the 1960 census had shown that the population of Blacks in New York City was second only to that in Johannesburg, South Africa. A huge population in the southern United States was living in conditions almost comparable to apartheid in South Africa. By the start of 1962, I had become much better informed and determined to work with those who wished to change society.

The YCW at St. Paul and Augustine's met regularly under the guidance of Father Gino Baroni, where we learned to evaluate conditions of the working man in a Christian society. We were a group of ten, growing to about fifteen, both male and female, Black and white, representing a variety of occupations and backgrounds. After a few meetings, it was decided that a local president should be elected, and I was selected. Probably some were concerned about a Protestant in a Catholic organization holding the position, but that was not the majority view. Prior to this time, my Christian commitments had lapsed, but now I decided to join a Washington Methodist Church, which was fully integrated. The minister welcomed me and I became a regular attendee.

In the spring of 1962, a Nigerian immigrant friend and I decided to make a trip into the southern United States to see if it was as bad as we had heard. A friend of Father Baroni lived in Asheville, North Carolina, so we selected it as our destination. Many people thought we were ridiculous, but we assured them that there were no plans to stage sit-ins at restaurant counters. We drove directly to North Carolina. When we stopped at restaurants, I went in and bought the food, and we ate in the car. The bathrooms, of course, were in the bushes. Arriving late at night in Asheville, there was no hotel available to us. In the end, we found a rather nasty, run-down, Black-owned hotel, but it was very enlightening, and after two days, we traveled back to Washington DC. On this return journey, we stopped at a Howard Johnson restaurant somewhere in Virginia, which accepted both of us.

I also became an active member of my trade union, the Meat Cutters. I attended meetings, acting as shop steward at the store, and was selected as a delegate to the DC Central Labor Council, where all matters affecting workers in the city were dealt with. This was an interesting group of people, covering a cross-section of the Washington area. Some unions were (and still are) segregated, some were struggling to correct the past, and others were predominantly Black. These were the hotel and restaurant workers, service employees, union people and laborers. The Bricklayers Union was split, with Blacks working on residential property and whites on commercial property. I soon associated with the delegates from the predominantly Black unions.

The dominating event for the United States and the world in 1962 was the Cuban missile crisis. The year before had included the Bay of Pigs fiasco, but I was still too new to the United States to fully evaluate those events. Now, I was more aware of the paranoia concerning Castro and his Communist Russian affiliation. To me, he was a freedom fighter comparable to Patrice Lumumba caught up in the U.S./ Russian rivalry, with both countries exploiting these leaders for their own political reasons. Castro had overthrown an evil dictator named Batista and freed poor Cubans, many of whom were Black. The Batista followers had fled to Miami, becoming a U.S. political force. Now I saw the two major powers of the world at loggerheads over this small country and on the verge of destroying the world. There was a genuine fear of these events throughout Washington and its citizens, including myself. Thankfully, it was brought to a conclusion, and we were able to continue our normal lives. However, the Miami Cubans never forgave President Kennedy and became die-hard Republicans. This, of course, suited their own racist background as the party started an association with the old Jim Crow Democrats.

My involvement with the Roman Catholic Church was helped by the appointment of Pope John XXIII, who modernized many facets of that religion. This did not mean I was ready to convert, but was ready to participate in all its procedures. I remained a Methodist, and above all, just a Christian. Father Baroni allowed me to participate in Catholic religious services, which would have been frowned on by many of his more conservative associates.

At the end of 1962, I took a two-week vacation back to England to celebrate Christmas with my family, who were pleased to see me and welcomed my renewed interest in Church matters. Some members of the Methodist Church, when discovering I had joined a Black church, said, "The choir must be wonderful." They thought every Black person sang like Paul Robeson. I did notice, in general, that there was much greater racism in British society as the Indian, Pakistani, and Black population had increased. It was nothing like the racist culture of the southern United States, however. The one thing that was very different was an equal resentment of people from the Indian subcontinent, who were classified as "Paks" for Pakistanis. It should also be noted that this population was only 1 percent of the total compared, to 11 percent for African-Americans in the United States.

1963 would prove to be one of the most depressing years and one of the most excitingly successful. In the southern states, Dr. Martin Luther King Jr. was mobilizing his Southern Christian Leadership Conference to great effect. These achievements were made due to the suffering of many Black Americans and some white Americans. These demonstrators were humiliated and abused by the Southern power structure, yet held to the principle of nonviolence. Thanks to the press, the world was able to see the evil of racial oppression in the United States. The Birmingham demonstrations were the most telling, and it became accepted by all concerned that this was the turning point in the civil rights movement.

1963 also saw the murder of Medgar Evers, and James Meredith's entrance into the University of Mississippi. We watched and read about these events with horror, and vowed the continuing aim of the YCW would be to change the system; our concentrations would be in Washington DC and surrounding areas. I attended memorial services for Medgar Evers at the Fourteenth Street AME Zion Church and his funeral at Arlington National Cemetery.

The YCW group aligned ourselves with CORE and joined picket lines in the F Street shopping center, where stores refused to hire Black salespeople. Our main assignment was at the Bowie Levittown housing development, where they maintained a standard of never selling houses to Black Americans. I spent many Sunday afternoons with my friends being verbally abused by the opposition. They stood there with a Confederate flag and yelled, "Two-four-six-eight, we don't want to integrate." Thankfully, the police presence stopped any chance of physical abuse. The Maryland police force was superior to its counterparts in Alabama.

I'm sorry to say we did not have an immediate effect, and Bowie waited for open-housing laws to come into effect before making any changes. Our efforts at St. Augustine's came to the attention of one of the television stations, and four of us appeared on a public interest show one Sunday morning. While it did not gather a huge audience, we would like to think it had some effect on the community.

As the year progressed, and the civil rights movement throughout the country gathered steam, A. Philip Randolph decided to work with others in planning a major march on Washington. He had done the same thing in the 1940s, placing pressure on President Roosevelt to open wartime jobs for Black Americas. This threat of a demonstration was somewhat effective—he realized that the time was ripe for an even bigger and better March in 1963. With his assistant Bayard Rustin and the cooperation of major trade unions such as the United Auto Workers Union, and all the civil rights groups, the plan went ahead. The date was set for August 28, and groups from all over the country planned to attend. Our YCW group joined in the organization in the Washington area, and my roommate and I volunteered to be official marshals at the event.

The official marshals for the March were under the direction of Julius Hobson, the head of CORE in the Washington area. We all met once a week for training and instruction on how to behave under all circumstances. It was emphasized that this was a nonviolent demonstration, and we vowed to commit ourselves no matter what their circumstances. During our training, we were continually photographed, and it was assumed that this was under the direction of the FBI, who cleared us all as suitable.

Other members of the YCW were involved in preparing accommodations for the thousands of visitors expected. Father Baroni was in direct contact with all the organizers on behalf of Cardinal O'Boyle, head of the Catholic Church in Washington DC. The cardinal promised to give his full support of the march, and just prior to the event nearly dropped out. He objected to a fiery speech that was to have been given by John Lewis, the head of SNCC. It was touch and go for a while. The compromise was reached, and the Catholic Church endorsed the march. Father Baroni, we believe, would have attended no matter what the cardinal said.

As the day of the march drew closer, there were several different reactions in the Washington area. Many white people said they were getting of the town, fearing a riot and something similar to Birmingham. Even a few Black Americans had a similar reaction, including my other roommate, who had always been very conservative. He took leave and went to visit friends in New York. The saddest one was a Black neighbor who said to me, "You don't understand those Southern coloreds."

My first problem was dealing with Safeway. I told them I was taking off to be a marshal at the march. The manager called an area supervisor to discuss it, and when I advised them that I would quit if they said no, they accepted my request. I will never know whether it was the union or the growing influence of the civil rights movement that changed their minds. My fellow employees, just said, "There he goes again."

The great day dawned, and my roommate Vince and I reported to the mall, close to the Washington Monument, where all the designated marshals assembled. We were given our final instructions and designated marching position. I was to proceed on the north side of Constitution Avenue. As we waited, the buses started to roll in. It was just amazing. There were hundreds of them. Thousands and thousands of people were assembling in Washington DC. As the crowd grew, we began to assemble outside of my group down Constitution Avenue, and we then cut through the trees in a shaded area next to the reflecting pool. While traveling to the march, there was no heckling, and most of the government workers cheered us as they stood outside their offices. It is interesting to note that at that time, Porta Johns were not readily available, and government offices opened their doors for toiletry uses.

We all assembled in our thousands, stretching from the Lincoln Memorial all the way back to the area, which is now the World War II Memorial. I had never seen a crowd this large. All were peacefully assembled with one goal of justice for all Americans of African descent. On the march, we must have sung "We Shall Overcome" twenty times and continued at the assembly. I will not go into the details all of the speeches made that day, culminating in the famous "I Have a Dream" speech by Dr. Martin Luther King. Needless to say, it was the most inspirational part of the whole day. Any reader can review the details from various sources, and

I strongly recommended the use of a video manufactured by the U.S. Information Agency detailing the events of the day. This can be obtained at the National Archives with payment for copying and the agreement not to use it for any commercial purpose.

At the end of the day, I was so excited and believed that this world for people of African descent in the United States was changed forever. This, of course, proved untrue, but there were some great changes. Some observations on the event and its supporters that struck me at the time were as follows: I was genuinely surprised at the number of white supporters who came to the demonstration. Until that time, I was under the impression that very few felt strongly about the issue of race. I thought they were mostly indifferent and very often negative.

Among the organizations that supported the march, several need recognition: United Auto Workers Union was among the strongest supporter from the AFL-CIO; other smaller unions with a large number of Black members obviously gave support; the DC's Central Labor Council, of which I was a member, voted to support the march. However, it should be noted that one of the representatives of the segregated construction unions stood up and said he supported the march because one of his favorite baseball players was supporting it. I would also note that the majority of Jewish organizations in the country supported the march, and many were in attendance on that day. This does not mean that a majority did not expound anti-Black sentiments. At that time in my life, I would have felt more comfortable in a room full of people of Jewish origin than an all-white Christian group.

People came in huge numbers from all over the country—the large cities on the East Coast, such as Boston and Philadelphia, and, above all, New York City. It was this group from New York City that impressed me the most. There were literally thousands upon thousands, and they probably formed a third of the attendees, ,from representatives from the giant Black community of New York to the old-line radicals like the Trotskyites and supporters of the Spanish Civil War revolutionaries.

The day after the march, I sensed a slightly different attitude from my white fellow-workers. They sensed relief that everything had gone off peacefully, and some admitted that I was right. Generally, throughout Washington, it was admitted that a new era had arrived for the months of September and October. There appeared to be a new appreciation that Black Americans had been denied their rights, and that something must be done. This can be traced directly to the Birmingham demonstrations in the spring and the march of August 28.

Dr. Martin Luther King Jr., with his striving for change though nonviolence, was given the credit for the improvements that were occurring both in attitudes and practical changes in the lives of many African-Americans. His popularity among both communities, Black and white, was enhanced by his comparison to Malcolm X and the so-called Black Muslims. They assisted in the development of the civil rights movements growing in Chicago, and then New York City as well as other northern cities. They claimed connections back to Africa and saw Islam as their natural religion. Some of these claims have questionable history, as the only group that could genuinely connect back to Africa and Islam were a group called the Beys. I met with some members of this group who could show a direct connection to his land. This should not detract from the influence that Malcolm X and the Nation of Islam had on the '60s, however. They represented the frustrations that a large number of Black Americans felt concerning their treatment, both in the Southern states and the North. Malcolm X was a very dynamic and influential speaker, but it should be noted that he rarely went to Birmingham or those other segregated Southern cities. To make militant speeches is easy when standing on the corner in New York or Chicago and talking about Black Power or what should be done to the white oppressors.

By the end of October, debate had started in Congress on the Civil Rights Act. It was pathetic to listen to some of the reports of the positions of Southern Democrats and even some of the more conservative Republicans from the north. A majority for the bill had not been counted on at that time, but we had hope. However, in November, what appeared to be a fatal blow was to strike the country and the world.

The assassination of President Kennedy was the very hardest blow to me and my friends and, perhaps, the whole nation. We were all convinced that it was motivated and organized by the Klu Klux Klan members and the Jim Crow south. This proved untrue, but conspiracy theories blossomed all over. This was further complicated by the assassination in public of his murderer. No one knew what would happen with President Johnson, a Southern Democrat from Texas. He proved us all wrong and became a strong advocate for the Civil Rights Legislation. In retrospect, I have to admit that the 1964 Civil Rights Act would never have passed without Johnson as president.

On the day of President Kennedy's funeral, our Safeway store was closed until one o'clock and, of course, I went downtown to view the event. It was very sad and exciting to view history taking place. The view that stands out in my mind is seeing a tall General de Gaulle and a very short Emperor Haile Selasie, marching together.

I returned to work, where the pithiest comment from a fellow employee was, what a shame for the family that this could happen at Thanksgiving. At least most people realized that this was a momentous event in history. I must admit that, along with others, I believed in a conspiracy sponsored by the segregationists. This was soon dispelled when events showed that it was some unknown individual with communist leanings. He was in turn assassinated on public television, giving rise to a world of speculation of conspiracies from that point on. Since that time, I have always been wary of conspiracy theories.

1963 came to an end with a new president; I was at first very suspicious of his commitment to civil rights for Black America. However, I was beginning to be proven wrong, as he seemed to continue to support our goals and bring along a few Southern Democrats. The YCW maintained its level of commitment to advancing the rights of Black Americans in Washington DC. My personal life started to change when, at a Christmas party, I met a young lady from Haiti who was to have a great impact on my life in 1964.

This year arrived and my life still revolved around work for YCW and its involvement in the civil rights movement within Washington DC and its suburbs. We followed events in the South, but as full-time workers, our participation was limited. Farther Baroni's friend, a minister at All Souls Unitarian Church, was killed at a demonstration. More famously, the death of the three civil rights workers in Mississippi occurred along with others. In Washington, our association with CORE continued, and we also joined with local leaders of SNCC, which included Stokely Carmichael and Marion Barry. They tried to organize a rent boycott at a poor apartment complex in the Parish, which was impractical as the people had nowhere else to go when evictions started. To me, this indicated the difference between idealistic students and the practical reality of urban life at that time.

After a long debate, and wrangling on Capitol Hill, the 1964 Civil Rights Bill was passed—due mostly to the efforts of President Johnson, who persuaded a few reasonable Southern Democrats to support it. In addition, moderate Republicans from the North gave their support as compromises were accepted. This bill and its implementation made a huge difference for many Black Americans in cities like Washington DC, Atlanta, and some border towns. I would estimate that the vast majority of white Americans in the Southern

States resented this law, but still accepted some compliance,. One of my fellow workers said, when he heard that the Gas Company now had Black meter readers, said, "See, they are taking our jobs." No matter how hard I tried, he could never understand that the denial of the jobs to Blacks had been wrong.

1964 was the year that the citizens of Washington DC got the right to vote for president. This was the capital of the United States, which prided itself as the bastion of democracy and freedom. I believed then and still do today that this denial was due in most part because 75 percent of the city was African-American. The YCW took an active part in registering people to vote for the first time. I clearly remember coming home after knocking on doors and asking people to register, and saying to Vince how sad I was that half the people agreed because the white man said to.

The presidential election proved an overwhelming success for President Johnson when he carried all the states except the Jim Crow South. His opponent ran for office as a conservative who believed in states' rights and opposed the Civil Rights Bill. There can be no doubt that the vast majority of Southern white votes were based on segregation. This move to the Republican party based on racial issues was to continue for many years to come.

At the end of the summer the YCW started to weaken— some either married or dropped out. Then I proposed to Gabrielle Richard, the Haitian woman I met at the Christmas party, and we planned our marriage for December 6 of that year. This was, of course, a momentous event when we announced it, as interracial marriages were not common at that time. Some of my friends at work suggested that I should leave the Fourteenth and U Street store, as there was a continuous negative attitude toward Blacks among the white employees. This coincided with the opening of the new International Safeway downtown, which I agreed to join. I became the manager of the Special Cheese Department. On arrival at the new store, I informed them of my marriage plans and said I would not tolerate any overt racism. On the whole, it was accepted, though I did not know what was said when my back was turned. It is interesting to note that the one openly Jewish employee continued to be derided, as if to say that David Palmer couldn't have everything.

On December 6, 1964, at St. Augustine's Church located at Fifteenth and V Street, Northwest, David Palmer married Gabrielle Richard—one born in England and the other in Haiti. In attendance were my brother, his wife and daughter Jane, as well as numerous members of the Richard family. Vince Deforest was my best man, and the church was full of friends and relatives. Both our families welcomed us with open arms. Those stories of interracial marriages causing family disputes did not occur here. My mother was concerned about religion based on that old English paranoia about the Pope, where so many older Protestants still thought the Catholic church wanted to reassert its authority. This was soon dispelled when we explained that Gabrielle's father was a leader in the Baptist Church, and his wife was Catholic.

Their marriage lasted for sixty years. I later heard that two of my cousins did not agree to the marriage, especially the one living in Rhodesia. They were no longer considered relatives.

The Richard family was part of what was known as the Black elite of Haiti. All were highly educated and successful in their careers. My father-in-law was an ex-cabinet member ambassador and now a prominent lawyer in Port Au Prince. In 1964 all relatives were out of politics and/or in exile as Papa Doc was in power. It proved an easy adjustment for me, even with my old radical background. Life in America for any Black family in the 1960s turned everyone to the left.

At the beginning of our marriage, we lived in a house with my wife's sisters and brother-in-law. It was fine, but a little crowded, and, by the end of February, we moved to our own home in the Brookland area of Washington DC. This was predominantly Black, and we adjusted easily, living there for six years.

1965 was a year of continuous struggle for civil rights in the Southern states. The most dramatic was the march in Selma, Alabama, led by Dr. King, culminating in a vicious attack by George Wallace's state troopers. The publicity related to this event culminated in the passage of the Voting Rights Act, which helped to correct the denial of voting rights to Black Americans. In Washington, our group of friends regularly picketed the White House until it was passed. We also appealed for home rule for Washington DC, but without success.

This was also the year of the buildup to the Vietnam War. After reviewing the facts concerning its goals and the threats to our society, I soon joined forces with those opposed. My friends and I joined demonstrations during the years of both the Johnson and Nixon administrations. This was a shame concerning Johnson, who proved an outstanding leader on the domestic front. I looked back to my days of opposition to the Suez crisis of 1956 and realized I had not changed so much. However, this war continued for years, killing so many people on both sides and achieving nothing. Working at the Safeway International during the initial years and seeing people buying nonstop. I could only compare it to England during World War II. Only the soldiers and their families experienced the suffering of Vietnam.

Chapter IV

As the reader would expect, marriage brought a great change in my life. My wife was well educated, but without a degree, which did not stop her from becoming secretary to one of the executive directors of the International Monetary Fund. At his appointment, she became the first Black secretary in the executive section ever. As you can see, the old segregated standards spread into the international organizations. My wife encouraged me to correct my own educational standards in order to move away from my limited future with Safeway. I obtained my old records from Malborough Grammar School and presented them to Goddard College of Plainfield, Vermont, where I enrolled in their adult degree program. I would receive a BA in three years.

The degree required that I attend the college for three weeks in both February and August each year. In between, I was to complete a major paper on my own initiative, but under the instruction of my professor. These were all at least fifty thousand words and original research; my resources were the DC Central Library, the Library of Congress, and through a friend, the University of Maryland Library. These were among my subjects: *The Failure of Marx to Affect Britain in the Nineteenth Century, The Development of the Supermarket in the U.S.; Haitian-U.S. Diplomatic Relations up to Occupation in the 1930s, Implementation of the United Nations Human Rights Act*, and *Anti-Black Racism Amongst Lower-Middle-Class White Americans*. Goddard was situated in a small town and appeared to be Plainfield's main industry. By the 1960's standards, it was classified as a liberal establishment catering to a Northeast elite who could not afford or qualify for a Harvard degree. The adult degree groups came from various places and were determined to make up for past failures. My first roommate was a retired general, which fascinated me after remembering my resentment of this social class in British society. The other who stood out in my memory was an ex-member of the Tuskegee Airmen. He only had a year to complete and we lost contact. Goddard gave me my first entry into a predominantly white American society where I could relax..

In 1965, our son Thierry was born, and he was joined by Vanessa in 1967. They brought great pleasure to our lives. Rearing children while studying and working was hard, but my wife and I managed somehow.

By 1967, with two years completed at Goddard, I applied for and was accepted as administrative assistant to the director of labor participation at United Nations Association. I achieved this in part due to my friends, my associations with the trade unions, and mostly a gentleman named Richard

Deveral, who had been the AFL-CIO representative in Japan after the war.

The director was James Carey, who had been Secretary Treasurer under the CIO prior to its merger with the AFL. Prior to this appointment, he had been president of the Electrical Workers Union but lost a disputed election. He was often considered a gadfly by the AFL-CIO's president, George Meany, but Walter Reuther of the UAW was a strong supporter. This move, on my part, was at first costly as a cut in salary was required from journeyman meat cutter. It proved a valuable steppingstone in my future. Mr. Carey was a fascinating character who taught me a huge amount of Union history in which he played a major role. The stories of the idiosyncrasies of other leaders from the past and the still-in-charge could have filled a book. His greatest idol was Phil Murray of the Steelworkers. Walter Reuther was in a high position and Carey was jealous of his success. There was no doubt that being an Irish Catholic was part of Careys success and rise to power.

In August 1967, I graduated from Goddard with my BA in history and economics and immediately enrolled at Howard University, seeking an MA. I enrolled for two courses per semester, which could be taken at night. My field of study was African American history and African government and history. I was one of the oldest students in the classes, but not the only white member. My grades were always A or B, but I did not graduate, because by 1969 my work requirements in a new job caused me to travel overnight on many occasions. One professor said, "You write nice papers, but you're never in class." My thesis study was never completed but the research was fascinating. My subject was Black participation in labor unions in Washington DC. I was able to interview many old Union members and read old copies of the *Afro American*, the *Washington Bee*, and the local *Trade Union Paper* back to 1902. To this day, I regret that many of my notes have been lost in house moving and the like. With the pressures of work, family, and continuous studying, I was ready to quit school.

1968 was a terrible year for a multitude of reasons; it appeared to be one tragedy after another. We entered with continuous frustration concerning the war in Vietnam. President Johnson kept sending more troops, but to no avail as the Viet Cong would never give up. Our generals were unable to deal with this kind of opposition, and one air force general said we were going to bomb them back to the Stone Age. Neither Johnson nor this secretary of defense had practical plans, and declared that pulling out was not an option. I like many people was saddened by Johnson's decision not to run again as his domestic policies were so good. Without the war, he would have gone down in history as one of our greatest.

In April, my wife took the children to visit Haiti and her parents. I could not go as visitors from the Russian United Nations Association were arriving on a special visit, and we were the official hosts. On the way back from the airport, after greeting the guests, I received devastating news on the assassination of Dr. Martin Luther King Jr. I went home to cry and felt very sorry for myself in an empty house. The next morning, the news brought the report of the reaction all over the country. There were people rioting and burning in the Black centers of all major cities. Washington was no exception and the fires could be seen as I went to work. I understood the reaction, but also realized, deep down, that it was not the answer. For the next few days I was busy with the Russians, showing them around the city and attending meetings. They were fascinated with what was happening with armed guards in front of the White House, government offices, and smoke billowing from Fourteenth street and other areas.

The Russians went home and Washington DC dealt with the aftermath of the events. Many sections were completely devastated and did not recover for years. I was familiar with Fourteenth Street from top to bottom; while traveling that road, I was saddened, but still understood why it happened. All the efforts of Dr. King to change our society peacefully had been attacked. However, life had to go on and the efforts to improve life for African-Americans continued. My old roommate, Vince, was active in the Poor People's March, which emphasized the huge extreme between the rich and poor. I supported all the efforts, but with school, family, and work was not as active.

After Johnson left the campaign, Hubert Humphrey and Bobby Kennedy competed for the Democratic nomination. I liked Humphrey, but his continuing support of the war pushed me to Kennedy. He seemed to be gaining momentum when yet another assassination ended all hope. All the conspiracy theories were rife, but it soon became clear that it was an individual nutcase. This was not true in regard to Dr. King, where all evidence pointed to a segregationist-appointed assassin. I am convinced to this day that he acted as directed by the Klan.

The Bobby Kennedy funeral took me back emotionally to 1963, and I wondered how many more of these events that family and the nation could endure. He was brought to Union Station and proceeded to Arlington, and there I was, standing on the sidewalk watching—but this time with my son at my side.

By September, the campaign for president between Humphrey and Nixon was heating up. I knew that Nixon was the worst possible opportunist, using every trick to gain support. He managed to appeal to the old segregationist South while vowing to uphold the law. Many of those Democrats were calling themselves Republican with Nixon's blessing. At first I held back from supporting Humphrey because of his continued support of the war. By October, my car had a Humphrey sticker, but it was too late, Nixon won. I still wonder whether people like myself handed over the country to the Republicans by our hatred for that war. We all knew that Nixon would be worse.

Nixon chose, as his vice president, Spiro Agnew, the governor of Maryland who had gained his office through an unusual route. His opponent had won the Democratic primary by using the phrase "Your home is your castle." He was, of course, appealing to the anti-Black sentiment concerning open housing. Decent Democrats and the large Black population switched to the lesser-known Republican Agnew, who took no position. This governor soon proved himself adept at taking advantage of every opportunity. He suited Nixon perfectly, as he was no threat to his power.

The inauguration came in January 1969. Along with a friend, I joined in an anti-Nixon demonstration, but it was already too late. I analyzed the situation with my life and status and decided to become a U.S. citizen. This was now my home and future; I had no special allegiance to England and the Queen. More than anything, I believed in the Bill of Rights and wished it could have been interpreted more effectively.

My United Nations Association lost its funding early in the year, and I immediately applied to the Federal Government, the then mainstay of employment for Washingtonians. A review of my background qualified me as an investigator for the Equal Employment Opportunity Commission. I was hired by the Washington District Office, which covered DC, Maryland, Delaware, Virginia, and West Virginia. The director was the first Black female to hold such a position in the Commission. She was tough and fair, insisting on quality work from her employees.

I worked hard and found myself traveling all over the area. Our responsibility was the implementation of Title VII of the 1964 Civil Rights Act, which meant, I had to investigate cases of employment discrimination based on race, sex, religion, and national origin. Most of the cases, at the start, were on race (Black) and sex, while religion and national origin were rare. The following are worthy of note:

In tobacco company cases in Richmond, Virginia, Blacks were hired into this industry and were members of the Tobacco Workers Union. Their jobs were in the preparation of the tobacco (dirty) while whites were in the finishing area, producing the cigarettes. I was involved in *Patterson v. American Tobacco Company*, which was fought through the courts by the NAACP and a local lawyer who later became the first Black mayor of Richmond.

I investigated a complaint of sex discrimination at a major hotel restaurant by a female employee who claimed males received better remuneration on service charges, and the union was also responsible. As a result of my efforts, policies were changed and the Waiters and Waitresses Union were merged.

I also became a successful conciliator of cases prior to any legal action. One of my most famous cases was in Parkersburg, West Virginia, where in 1962, all the women in the fiberglass plant were laid off. In 1968, the company started to rehire employees. The women wanted to be rehired, but the company claimed the law was not in effect in 1962, and that they had no claim. The company was ready to go to court, but agreed to pay compensation and rehire as needed if I could find all the women on the roster and they sign the agreement. Those who filed the complaint agreed to the terms, but I had to find the others. I traveled all over the Parkersburg area and found them. There was a signed agreement with fifty signatures based on my efforts. I knew this was only possible in West Virginia in 1971.

In Norfolk, Virginia, I spent weeks at a huge shipyard investigating and settling cases. For a while, the Tidewater area became my second home. This area had a large Black population with the adjoining county of Stafford being 50 percent Black. The remnants of slavery still existed, with identical last names for both Black and white. Virginia was an eye-opener regarding the remnants of slavery and Jim Crow. Working conditions in some areas were appalling—far below anything in Western Europe, where such treatment would have been illegal. In settling a case at a non-union steel plant in Lynchburg, I found no sick leave for the victim, and when asked for back pay during Christmas through New Year, the management explained that every Christmas Eve, they laid people off, and rehired January 2. These terms applied to all employees and were not a violation of Title VII.

I advanced quite rapidly at this office and soon became a senior investigator and conciliator. In addition, I was elected the office EEO officer who dealt with internal complaints. This was a great compliment, but often proved thankless when one older lady complained that a male had touched her inappropriately. The whole issue made no sense but caused friction for weeks. It was resolved and we could laugh about it later. I lost this unwanted position when the director made me a supervisor. It should be understood that supervising and directly working with people who dealt with employee complaints caused adverse reactions, personally. One that stands out was an annual evaluation procedure. For example, the director required that all sections must be completed, including "Needs for improvement." One of my employees was a sixty-year-old who had been in the government for years, and no one had ever mentioned such a thing to her. She was in tears in my office, but I held my ground, knowing what I said was correct. By 1972, I could proudly say that I had found the profession that suited me.

The Palmer family made a big decision in February 1970 when they moved to a new house. My wife wanted our son to attend French school in the Tenleytown area, and she could not drive, so we bought a new house close by. This was a richer, predominantly white area, but open housing was now in effect. I made the first inquiries and brought my wife to see the house after the price was established. We moved in, and the neighbors to our right put their house on the market immediately. The other neighbor did not speak for two years, but the rest accepted us. Washington in 1970 was not perfect; however, it had gotten to be a lot better than 1961 for middle-class Blacks.

The other big change came in the structure of local government. The Voting Rights Act brought a change in Congress and, naturally, in the District Committee. The old Jim Crow Democrats were weakened and the appointed commissioners were replaced by an appointed mayor and city council. After a few years we were granted the right to vote for mayor and council. It took the 1970s for democracy to be granted to the capital of the "free world." We even got a congressman (who sat on committees and had no vote on the floor). However, the District Committee still existed with veto power over our laws. The Council had a chairman and twelve members, and they slipped in a clause that two members could not be from the majority party, which resulted in the set-aside for the Republicans. Just imagine, the Republican party had its own Affirmative Action program.

I still opposed the war and Nixon's handling of it. He had not opposed any of the Civil Rights changes but managed to gather around him many who had. The Republican party was starting to become the white male stronghold. Whenever the administration was criticized, it jumped on the bandwagon that it was the liberal Eastern media's fault. They sent out Agnew to belabor the point, and somehow he intimidated many sections of the press. There were journalists on the radio stating they were from the Midwest. The worst were the statements made by the *Washington Post*, which seem to bend over backwards to find semi-conservative positions. They seemed to modify their support for civil rights and definitely supported the war in Vietnam. Later in the Nixon years, they regained some of their credibility, but in my opinion, still proved themselves moderate rather than liberal.

In 1973, an opportunity arose whereby I could join a special investigation unit at EEOC Headquarters on a national program. We were divided into four groups covering various industries. I was appointed second in command to a group covering the International Brotherhood of Electrical Workers and the Electrical Contractors Association. The group leader had been recruited from the Department of Labor and knew nothing about Title VII. The director, David Copus, had designated leaders based on ethnic, sexual, and racial groups, and not necessarily knowledge. Copus himself had solid legal ability in the implementation of Title VII.

This was my first exposure to control by diversification. In addition, the growing importance of Hispanics as an aggrieved minority now came to my attention. I discovered the broad definition troubling as anyone who had a Spanish last name or ancestry was covered. One of the ex-district office employees named Santiago Rodriguez had a Puerto Rican father and German mother, and was blond and blue-eyed, but was now strongly Hispanic. In the old office, when he discovered my English background, he talked nonstop about his German roots—now they were forgotten. Let's face it, he could have gone anywhere in the Jim Crow states in the 1950s.

The investigations started and we gathered information from all over the country where complaints had been filed. This was analyzed by the staff of four in my group and stockpiled in preparation for a decision. Compared to my work at the District Office, it was easy, and two of us could have completed it all. This was my first taste of bureaucracy for its own sake. The group leader thought his only role was to make militant statements that would impress the Black employees. When I discovered that the local apprenticeship program in San Francisco was in compliance, he called them bastards—as if it were an affront to our goal of finding fault. After one year, I made the decision to return to the District Office. This was a valuable experience in some ways, and the efforts that were made by this organization brought publicity to our goals and made most employers show respect for the law.

I returned to my position as supervisor of investigations and conciliations as the District Office. We had a new director, named Treadwell Phillips, and our jurisdiction covered Washington DC and Virginia as Maryland and Delaware came under the new Baltimore office. Not only did I train new investigators, but I carried a full workload as well. One interesting development was the introduction of pre-decision settlement. We could now approach a respondent about settlement prior to making a decision. I settled many cases this way and saved a lot of time for both sides, as the office had a huge backlog of complaints. There were many characters in the office, but the most unusual was a Black woman who had a law degree, stuttered badly, and had converted to Judaism, where she sang in the Synagogue choir. With all this, she proved a hopeless investigator no matter how hard I tried to teach her.

During this period, I observed that Title VII was having an impact on employment for African-Americans. Employers, however reluctant, were trying to comply. Sex discrimination was still not understood. In one case, a company wrote me, saying, "We laid off both the Black women and the white women." Most of the company's representatives resented complaints being filed and claimed absolute purity. The best-remembered situation was the lawyer who wrote on behalf of his client that as he was Irish, discrimination was impossible, but provided no evidence concerning the issue. I felt like reminding him that Savannah, Georgia, was 50 percent Irish, and Jim Crow had reigned supreme for many years.

An interesting change in race relations during the 1970s was instituted by television comedy. A program called *All in the Family* made fun of Archie Bunker, who was an open bigot. So many people did not want to admit that such bigotry existed, though deep down they knew. Making a fool of Archie did more to challenge such values than many so-called community counseling sessions ever could. I attended one of these groups, but was asked to leave when I told a retired priest he had a problem. This man said he served in the navy during World War II and knew nothing about race discrimination. During the war, the Navy was completely segregated as Blacks were confined on all ships to Galley as cooks and servants.

The Nixon administration went through continuous turmoil, starting with the war in Vietnam and concluding with the shame of Watergate. I made note of my observations at that time. Henry Kissinger as national security advisor and later secretary of state ran the war with Nixon. Both were Cold War warriors, and Nixon had a long history of using anti-Communism as a tool against the opposition. They could not give in and settle this hopeless war, so it dragged on and on. Then they shook us all by recognizing Red China. For years, this country of a billion people was outlawed by the U.S., and anyone who suggested recognition was blasted as a soft pink communist sympathizer. Nixon did it and no one could complain. At the same time, they were overthrowing the elected government of Chile and replacing it with a right-wing dictator. By the 1972 election, the administration was becoming so paranoid that they bugged the Democratic offices at the Watergate Hotel. It was a second-rate burglary and an indication to what lengths they would go to win. The first to go was Vice President Agnew, when it was discovered he was embroiled in corruption while serving as governor of Maryland. He was replaced by Ford, who President Nixon saw as no threat to his power. Johnson had stated that Ford could not walk and chew gum at the same time.

President Nixon resigned and Vice President Ford replaced him. Though no great shakes, he gave stability to the country and integrity to the presidency. I was not sad to see President Nixon go, but could not question his ability; if only it had been applied in an honorable form. His administration did not repeal the Civil Rights laws and, on the whole, supported their implementation. However, within the Republican party, there was a growing use of appeals to the racist past. Many white males saw the Democrats as appealing to Black needs and voted against their old party. In addition, there was a growing fundamentalist Christian movement that joined the right wing of the party. They were not openly racist, but knew how to appeal to that past. Billy Graham became a great supporter of Nixon, and those to his right even more so. I cannot forget that Graham had accomplished nothing to help Dr Martin Luther King Jr. He had come to England in the 1950s and tried to convert us to his way, and yet, there appeared to be no evidence that he ever condemned segregation.

During the 1970s, the Palmer family regularly visited England and Haiti. We were welcomed in Aldbourne, though an undercurrent of racism did seem to exist. Our son reported some arguments with one boy, but his prowess as a soccer player kept him popular. In Haiti at that time, I had no problems except for continuous begging. The white man from overseas represented money, but Haitians under Papa Doc were not very aggressive. It was, of course, my first exposure to the Third World. I had read of the conditions, but it still shocked me to see it firsthand. My wife's family were higher up the social scale, but were not exploitive of their position.

Nixon and probably the worst of his administrators left with him. Ford took Rockefeller as his vice president, signaling the return of the more moderate northeastern wing of the Republican party. Thankfully, the Vietnam War came to an end, even if it was in an inglorious fashion.

Chapter V

At the end of 1976, a lawyer who represented several complainants at the Commission, as well as respondents, recruited me for an outside position. Willie Leftwich was a Black Republican whose firm was counsel to the Deleuw, Cather and Parsons group contracted to run the rebuilding of the railroad tracks between Washington and Boston. This was a 2.5 billion dollar project in a time when a billion dollars meant something. They had a contractual requirement of a 28 percent minority employment goal. The Department of Transportation, which had a Black secretary, William Coleman, the first in any Cabinet, insisted with his staff on his high goal and the selected contractor who agreed to it. They insisted that these goals were to be met across the board, and not only secretarial.

Attorney Leftwich insisted that I was the only person he knew with the ability to do the job. At first, there was some reluctance to have a white man in the position, and my interviewers were skeptical. I was approved by the project director, the federal railroad administrator, and finally Parsons, Vice President, in Washington DC. He had wanted his secretary, a Black woman, in the job. I agreed to take her as assistant director, as I could tell she was very skilled, though with limited knowledge of EEO laws. Vice President Volpe was a major force in Parsons and headed a major Washington DC law firm. He was of the old school in Washington DC and did not really believe in the program. His one question to me was, "Aren't White people a minority in DC?" I knew this man would not be my major supporter.

I met with the project director, an old railroad man who came out of West Virginia and still owned a farm in the western suburbs of DC. Based on his background, I would have guessed this was not my best friend. I could not have been more wrong. He was 100 percent behind me and let every manager knew that they should support me, or else. I took a firm stand with all the mangers and subcontractors and informed them that I meant business. DCP was going to meet the 28 percent goal or else. I first had to deal with definitions. Under the law that appropriated the money for the project, "minority" included women. This meant that white women would easily, with others, make the goal. FRA and my director supported me in separating Caucasian women statistically. Affirmative Action continued, encouraging all women for promotions and hiring into top professional positions. On a personal basis, I did not think this broad definition of minority was the best way to correct the long history of denial to African-Americans, but I was a professional and implemented the law as it was written.

Current employees of the Parsons organization trans-
ferred from California, and most of them were white, with a
smattering of Asians and Hispanics. My job looked impossible, but at least the Deleuw employees, who were based
in Washington DC, included Blacks. The Parsons managers
were amazed to hear me and what I expected, but reluctantly
agreed to cooperate. The most interesting aspect of Parsons'
employment record was a history of always hiring from the
military. We had generals, colonels, and even an admiral in
all departments. My biggest nemesis was the head of Contracts, a retired air force general who resented my interfer-
ence in his special empire. I won several sorties and I often
thought of my days as a corporal in the RAF. The first Black
professional hired for Parsons worked in the Environmen-
tal Department. His name was Thurlow Tibbs, who later in
life became the greatest collector and consultant for African
American art. He told me that Bill Cosby and Oprah Win-
frey became his clients.

The other affirmative action program was for minority-
owned business. This had developed under the Nixon administration with the hope that small Black-owned businesses
would help pull people out of the ghetto and give rise to
an entrepreneurial middle class. DCP hired a Black-owned
firm from New York to recruit such businesses to meet some
goals, like mine. The company had four Black employees
on the job, which boosted my statistics in the first year. We
worked together, but I always knew that their role was always
more important to FRA and management than mine. Our
two offices had a good relationship supporting mutual goals.

Some other managers thought my job was subsidiary to the other, but I asserted myself strongly and maintained power. I look back now and wonder what happened to that meek teenager.

Ford lost the 1976 election and Jimmy Carter was inaugurated in January 1977. As a convicted Democrat, I was pleased, but a little wary of a Georgia governor and so-called born-again Christian. But Carter proved himself worthy, and progress was made in the next four years. This does not mean that racism against African-Americans was eliminated, but there was genuine improvements. There still remained a large number of Black Americans at the bottom on the ladder.

On a personal level, one change in my life in the 1970s centered around soccer. My son, at the age of six, showed himself to be a good athlete, and I started to train him in the game. With some trepidation on my part, he joined a team in suburban Montgomery County. He was accepted immediately, and I helped with the coaching on verbal basis. I had never been a good player, but loved and understood the game. He progressed over the years with select teams throughout the suburban area. When he was ten, his team played a team from Bowie, which they won. It felt good when I thought back to the years when I picketed this community. During the same period, Washington gained its own professional soccer team. I became friendly with the management and conducted a survey for them concerning youth participation in the metropolitan area. In addition, I was able to obtain a signed photograph of Henry Kissinger, which hung in their office for many years.

The Carter administration, in those early years, proved a breath of fresh air, cementing the gains from the Johnson years. He also delivered an enlightened international policy. First he brought a major peace treaty between Israel and Egypt, then followed up by attempting to quell the unrest in Iran. However, this got out of hand, and the fundamentalist Muslims joined with the left-wing students to overthrow the Shah. These groups blamed the United States and took Embassy diplomats hostage. They freed the Black staff members, thinking this would please the Black community in the United States. There was no evidence to support this view, and the hostage situation brought about the downfall of Carter and heralded something worse. ABC's *Nightline* started to count the days the diplomats were being held hostage, which held Carter hostage in the White House. The Iranians jumped on the opportunity to humiliate him as much as possible. An attempt by the U.S. Military failed to rescue anyone, and the president had to take the blame for their inefficiency. The right wing of the Republican party jumped on the bandwagon and the administration's fate was sealed.

This was the start of the Arab/Islamic revolution, which continues today. With the oil boycott and Iran, they destroyed the only reasonable president for sixteen years and brought untold misery on themselves as well as their perceived enemies.

My work at DCP, until 1980, continued with a modicum of success. The 28-percent goal was being met by the main management force. However, I have to admit that this was helped by the broad definition of "minority." People from Asia and the subcontinent of India were now classified, as well as anyone with a Spanish surname. Engineers from India were often more common than some white Americans on our application forms. I continued to push for more Black recruits, but could not discriminate against other minorities. One Jamaican-born employee of Chinese/Black parentage insisted on being classified as Asian.

In 1978, we were contracting for final design companies and, of course, recruiting for minority businesses. At times, this caused problems for my program when such subcontractors did not comply. Most notable was a Delaware architectural company owned by a Cuban immigrant. He employed no minorities on his contract, at any time. When he came up for a second contract, I protested, but was overruled. The other problem was with women-owned businesses: when a husband handed over 51-percent ownership to his wife, it became a minority business. The majority of Black-owned businesses had a good record on employment, although one did report only one African-American (himself). For all these problems, goals were met, and in the summer of 1980, we employed ten Black interns from Howard University who worked in all departments of the company. In addition, a contract worth a million dollars was awarded to the Urban League to study minority employment in the Northeast.

1980 brought the end of the Carter administration under inglorious terms and heralded a man who appeared pleasant, but was controlled by the worst sections of the Republican party. Carter had brought peace between Israel and Egypt, amnesty to the wounds of Vietnam, and hope to many of the poorest in the country. He was not always perfect, but I missed him when he left office.

Reagan was elected by appealing to some of the worst sections of our voting public. First and foremost, he appealed to the Christian Right, which had its origins in the old South. Such leaders as Jerry Falwell out of that wonderful town of Lynchburg (just imagine the origin of that name). Yes, they had a few Blacks in the choir, but the theme was fundamental evangelism, not social justice. Reagan even made the statement that he knew nothing about racism and segregation. This was a man who grew up in the Midwest, provided commentary on baseball, and came to fame in Hollywood, where most Blacks played maids and other servants. Needless to say, he led an administration that promoted the idea that a little racism was okay.

At work, this atmosphere spread from the FRA toward DCP, and I had to redouble my efforts to promote affirmative action in employment. I was fortunate that my immediate management supported me. A new director was appointed who had retired from the Air Force to NASA for twenty years before joining Parsons; he gave me reassurance, and I grew to respect him. This was a man who could manage an organization firmly.

We started to subcontract for final construction and I was able to maintain the goal on most of these projects. We visited the sites and oversaw the compliance. Two reviews are of interest. At a toxic removal company in Delaware, all employees maintained protective gear only to have their subcontractor truck drivers not comply—all of whom were white. I stood aside from that one. At the Newark station, we removed asbestos, and, safety controls were in effect. However, our site manager telephoned me to say I should investigate the fact that all the employees were Black in this hazardous job. I had to explain to him that if regulations were complied with, no one was going to tell employees making $17 per hour to leave. His heart was in the right place and he so wanted to please me.

By 1983, all construction came under the control of Amtrak, and minority business contracts were accepted. Their MBO insisted that I had no control over any MBE concerning employment, and this was supported by FRA. The end result was that these contractors had no concern with employment. The most horrendous case was a painting contract of a bridge in New Jersey, where the owner handed over the ownership to his wife; when the reports came, every employee was a white male with an Eastern European name. Another contract on a high bridge near Boston allegedly hired Mohawk Indian employees, who were famous for having no fear of heights. All employees came from an area near Canada and tribal areas. The addresses were given as proof, but they had standard American names and looked like standard white males.

We did exceed our goals on most contracts, and our office was proud of the achievements. By 1985, the project was moving toward closure and I assumed more responsibilities for minority business contracts for Parsons with other governmental agencies. This was a new direction for me, but the federal government was no longer interested in employment programs. We had several successes; however, in the end, the company considered my input unneeded when I suggested a 15 percent goal, and the agency said 5 percent was enough. In November 1986, I separated from Parsons with my integrity intact; the goals, which at the beginning were thought to be impossible, had been met. I started yet another career, as a consultant to a minority-owned engineering firm, and also obtained a license as a commercial real estate agent.

The Reagan administration ruled us until 1988; they had a president who followed directions and presented his speeches perfectly. I did not like these policies but will admit that the people in charge were brilliant in promotion and delivery. The country was made to feel good about itself, and anyone who questioned policies was considered unpatriotic. No one could ever question a president who was a nice guy, and had I known him personally, I may have agreed.

First and foremost, Reagan will be remembered for the collapse of the Soviet Union. His policy of emphasizing military power against his so-called evil empire hastened their demise. They could not compete and it bankrupted their government. Even before this time, they had lost badly in Afghanistan and the horror of Chernobyl. The arrival of Gorbachev as leader made collapse possible. This man obviously could see it was impossible and knew their economic and governmental system did not work—I would even question whether any of these so-called leaders back to Stalin ever believed in it. Probably the last real Russian Communist was Trotsky.

Of special interest to me was the friendship between Reagan and Thatcher. I did not like either, as they represented their right-wing political parties, but they were still an odd couple. She was a tough ruler in direct control of her administration, while he had plenty in the White House telling him what to do. She was probably his intellectual superior who portrayed him as an equal, realizing where the power in the world lay. Besides the collapse of the Soviet Union, the lesser known joint venture was the Falklands (Malvinas) war; I have on good authority that weapons used by the British were, for the most part, supplied by the U.S. This commitment, dating back to World War II, where one country always supported the other, has consequences up to today.

The assassination attempt on Reagan took everything back to Kennedy—conspiracy theories were rampant. A careful review soon showed it was another nutcase, which our society creates at regular intervals.

Perhaps the greatest failure of the Reagan administration was on foreign policy dealing with the Middle East. He had come to power based on his belief that his administration would stop similar Iranian events. Then two hundred marines were killed during the massacre in Lebanon, which resulted in a pullout. This was followed by Iran-Contra, where we sold out our principles to the very people who had taken our Embassy employees hostage.

I was glad to see him go and hoped a more reasonable Republican administration under George Bush Sr. might be possible. The election campaign pitted Mondale and the first female vice presidential candidate for the Democrats. Bush chose as his running mate an unknown senator from Indiana named Quayle, who was no threat to his authority. Quayle soon proved himself an embarrassment to Bush by his limited ability and his failure to spell "potato" in a public forum. The campaign soon showed that the old guard of the Republican party was still in control when they openly appealed to the anti-Black segment of the public. An advertisement showed a Black criminal who had been paroled, conveying the idea that if you vote Democrat, this is what you will get.

The main feature of the Bush administration was, of course, the Gulf War. This occurred right after the fall of the Soviet Union, and Bush was able to bring all forces together in the fight. There were many theories as to why we fought, but the basic issue was an unprovoked attack on a sovereign state. Some of my friends wondered why I did not oppose this war, as they thought of me as semi-pacifist. In fact, I saw this as closer to World War II; Kuwait was Poland, and Saddam had to be stopped. So, the United States, with the support of the world, won. War is not nice and should be avoided, if possible. This time it could not. On the whole, the Bush administration did a good job. I did attend the Victory March in Washington, but cringed sometimes at the overt nationalism.

In the period from Reagan to Bush, Washington DC saw the rise of a new mayor, Marion Barry. I knew him from the past and voted for him right from the beginning. He made great changes to the city and, in my opinion, mostly good. Moving DC government offices to the outer, predominantly Black areas was first and foremost. The Reeves Center at Fourteenth and U Streets, along with the subway station located at Thirteenth Street, has made the area a top financial section. Marion had his personal problems, and some of his business associates raised questions. This was nothing compared to the days of appointed commissioners of the '50s and '60s, who promoted businesses based on whims of racist congressmen.

The other big change to DC during the '70s and '80s was a large drop in population. This was due, in the most part, to the flight of many middle- and upper-income Black Families. Grandmothers and grandfathers stayed behind while people with children moved. All suburban areas gained, but the biggest gain was to Prince George's County. Blacks soon became the majority there for most income groups. Now we saw sections like Mitchellville becoming the home of rich Blacks. Some called it the new Gold Coast, which was the name given the rich Black area on Sixteenth Street during the 1950s and 1960s.

I had now entered my new career as a commercial real estate agent, where I was relatively successful and also prospered from some wise investments. The reader will speculate that I had become a complete capitalist. In my heart, I maintained my socialist roots even though fast becoming a cynic in regards to Christianity. Pat Robertson and Jerry Falwell de-converted me.

The two firms I was associated with were Jewish-owned and predominantly staffed. They accepted me as one of their token goys, but showed some concern with my pro-Black position. At several staff meetings, it was necessary for me vehemently attack racist statements. The brokers always apologized afterwards, but it was obvious that their positions did not change when I wasn't there. Any idea that Jews were above racism was soon shattered by these experiences. Also, I was back in the real world, no longer sheltered by my position as an EEO officer. It was not as hard as the 1960s, and middle-class Blacks were now accepted, but those poor ones were kept at arm's length. I did have one advantage over some of the white salespeople, in that I would sell in Black areas of the District of Columbia.

This new career, though not a dynamic success, did prove quite profitable and was enhanced by the purchase of two properties at reasonable rates. One commission sale was of interest because it brought back my previous work in minority business. I represented this minority construction company in DC in buying a new warehouse. The company classified as Hispanic was owned by a man who spoke Portuguese; when I asked him where he came from in Brazil, he said, "No, I came directly from Portugal.". I did not say anything, but couldn't help thinking this was not the purpose of the civil rights laws.

In 1989, I made an overseas trip that had a lot of meaning for me. This was a two-week visit to Zimbabwe and, of course, my first to Africa. The tour included Harare, Bulawayo, Victoria Falls, a safari park, and the Aswan Dam. I knew my long-lost cousin, who had avoided me for years, lived there. I found him in the telephone book, and he was so pleased to meet me when he realized I was on my own. He invited me to his club and even flew me in his private plane. He was now a manager for Ericson, which gives you a good idea about affirmative action for white Englishmen going to Rhodesia in the 1950s. In 1989, Mugabe was president and the old apartheid system was part of the past. Everyone in government referred to each other as "Comrade," implying some kind of socialist or communist government, but the Harare Stock Exchange flourished. I met a lot of interesting people and at that time saw a great future for the country. Some of the visitors in my group included white South Africans who were confused by my continuous friendship with Africans only. They invited me to visit South Africa, but I soon informed them that I wouldn't fit.

Bush seemed to destroy himself even after a great success with the Gulf War, and Bill Clinton was elected. One of the reasons for the victory was the rival campaign of Ross Perot, who drained off some Republican votes. In other words, the Republican party was still a strong force in the country and Congress. They used this power to attack and try to destroy Clinton at every turn. He was criticized for being a draft dodger during the Vietnam War when he was against the war on principle; this to me made him a man of honor and integrity. This sniping on every issue continued throughout his presidency, and in my opinion made the Republicans even more objectionable than when they were in the White House.

The new administration brought more stability to the economy and the country prospered, bringing down the national debt. This was achieved while reemphasizing social issues and helping all people at the bottom of the ladder. The African-American community felt that they now had a president who understood their standing in the country. After the Democrats lost their majority in Congress, the changes Clinton sought were curtailed—most notably, the effort under his wife's direction, a national health service. Once more, the people on the bottom income classes lost out.

In foreign policy, he had to deal with the breakup of Yugoslavia and specifically Kosovo. This meant working with NATO and Europe, in which he did a reasonable job during an impossible situation. The new British prime minister, Tony Blair, became an ally, and on the whole, American was popular in Europe. Clinton was also very popular in Africa, where he was considered a friend to the new South Africa.

The fall of apartheid in South Africa was, in fact, the most important event of the 1990s, in my estimation. Watching Nelson Mandela with his wife, as they walked out of jail, had a strong emotional impact on me. This was followed by his election as president, and, I started to feel that the world was becoming a better place. I remembered at the time that I had actually considered going to South Africa in 1960 instead of the United Sates. In retrospect, I believe that had I landed in Pretoria instead of Washington DC, my life would have been very different. In fact, had I behaved the same way, I would probably have been dead or in jail.

Washington DC in the 1990s went through Marion Barry twice as mayor and its first female, Patricia Harris. Barry's second term ended abruptly due to his arrest on drug charges. This was a great pity, as I liked him, and I still believe that his addiction was more to do with the women, than the drug. The new mayor came from an establishment Black background and everyone had high hopes. However, she seemed to flounder in dealing with the bureaucracy and the City Council and left after one term. Back came Barry, to the amazement of the country, which used him unfairly to criticize the DC electorate. Suburbanites, then and since, always make unfair assumptions that the DC government is incompetent. People made claims that nothing in DC operated efficiently, yet they had never used our facilities. Like any other big city, things would go wrong, but no more so than New York, Los Angeles, or other major cities. Tony Williams replaced Barry, and there was an upsurge in the economy and our status. A lot of credit must be given to Williams, but he was also fortunate regarding the huge increases in property values and property sales, which swelled the city's revenue.

After eight years, the Clinton presidency came to an end and the new millennium began. Clinton had proved himself a very good leader who had been hampered by the Republican majority in Congress. In addition, the failure to deal with his extramarital relationship presented a problem. He should not have succumbed to a very determined young woman but when he did, he admitted it. At the end of the twentieth century, the USA was the only country in the Western world that considered such an event a crisis.

George W. Bush. was elected on a disputed vote that was finally decided by a Republican Supreme Court. I did not like it, but accepted reality and hoped for the best when Bush appointed Colin Powell as secretary of state and spoke of compassionate conservatism. This indicated some hope for the future, but we were to be sadly disappointed. With Cheney as vice president, Rumsfeld at the Pentagon, and an attorney general who was a religious nut, I should have known better.

The African-American community was impacted by two events during this transition of one century to the next. The Nation of Islam, which had lain dormant for many years, was rejuvenated by the rise of a new leader, Louis Farrakhan. Like Malcolm X, he came out of a questionable background, not related to social/political activism. He was able to make the country aware. Black America was not satisfied with its lot. He organized the Million Man March in Washington DC. The number that attended is disputed, but the fact that so many came emphasized the point that all was not well in the community. It was not comparable to the March on Washington in 1963 and was soon forgotten three months later. However, Farrakhan became a name associated with Black frustration. The other event that caught the headlines in this period was the trial of O. J. Simpson. He may have been guilty, but the prosecution was a complete failure. Once again, he raised strong support in the Black community, much to the frustration of white society. These feelings of dissatisfaction brought out by these two men reminded us all that the evils of the past against the African world were not forgotten.

In the year 2000, I started to plan for my retirement, which would be one year away. I had been relatively successful in real estate, was not under great financial pressure, and worked only half days in the office with occasional meetings in the afternoon, accordingly. It had been an interesting career with clients from all over the world as well as American; they included people from India, Korea, Ethiopia, Afghanistan, Iran, and China, and, of course, African-Americans. In 2001, I retired from the Jewish-owned company, but kept my license and listed with an African-American company I had started to associate with for the previous six months. It was very a very loose relationship, as for all intense and purposes, I was not working, but visiting the office once a week. The only other work was managing a property I owned.

In August 2001, I was diagnosed with prostate cancer and, after careful evaluation, chose radiation treatment, enrolling in a program with the National Cancer Institute. This was based at the Bethesda Naval Hospital and NIH. The radiation was combined with a series of shots that was believed to tell the cancer to go away. This covered a miserable six months, but as of today, I am cancer free. I just wish I did not have incontinence and continuous tiredness.

On September 11, 2001, our world changed. My wife became a U.S. citizen on that day, and the events unfolded as we were rushed out of the courthouse and drove home. It was unbelievable for all Americans, and I can only evaluate it rationally well after the event. It was obvious that Bush did not know what to do at that time. The Arab Muslim world was also confused; where some groups cheered, others were saddened and knew this was not the answer. The world was now reaping the results of bad policies on both sides, from Suez to the present.

The war in Afghanistan was probably the right policy for the Bush Administration. They were succeeding in trying to control a country that was completely out of control, but could not leave it at that and decided to finish what Father Bush had failed to do in Iraq. I am not a pacifist, but believe in avoiding war at all costs. It appeared from the start that the U.S. and Britain were going to war with Iraq no matter what, and they presented evidence to back up the reasons. I did not join any peace rally and watched Colin Powell and Tony Blair, who I admired, hoping they were right. What a sad situation. It became a war ill advised and badly run.

The next tragedy of the Bush administration was Katrina. The television coverage of that event did not need commentary. It showed continuous incompetence and indifference on the part of the administration. We saw a huge poor Black population who had no resources abandoned by those in power, and I thought the 1960s were not far away. The rest of the world saw an exposure of the United States as a Third-World power. Iran had done a better job during its last earthquake. I realized that the Bush administration, with its handling of Katrina and its Iraq policy, was the worst administration since Harding in the 1920s.

In 2002, the DC Historical Society opened a museum covering the history of Washington DC at the old Carnegie Library building. I visited the museum and fell in love with its presentation. I immediately volunteered to act as docent once or twice a week. With all modesty, I can claim to have been a success in this role. I had lived and worked in the city since 1961, knowing all its political and historical ramifications. The main section, called Perspectives, had an aerial view of the city on the floor, and I could find nearly every street better than most taxi drivers. Sadly, the museum closed after three years, due to poor support. The main reasons were the reluctance of Washingtonians to pay for entrance (the Smithsonian is free), lack of publicity, and bad press by the *Washington Post* and other newspapers. After closing, the building remained open for special events, and I performed as docent for many of these, such as the Black Caucus and event parties for George W. Bush's inauguration in 2005. I met some fascinating people at these occasions, and all of them enjoyed the museum. Now it is closed; the presentation has been removed completely and replaced with a music center.

At this time, I am concluding my memories, as everything now is having an immediate impact.

Chapter VI

The final chapter will cover general observations of groups and organizations in the society I have lived. As the reader will expect, the overwhelming theme of my life and philosophy is that in the United States, "Race Black, is always a factor". This section should also be prefaced by the phrase, "Some of my best friends are ..." In other words, my criticism does not include all members of a group or race.

The history of African-Americans in the United States from the beginning to the late twentieth century can only be described as horrendous. These are just the basics:

African slavery and trade was unique and in some ways more reprehensible than any other. The usual pattern had been that a victor in battle took prisoners home as slaves. The Europeans chose to raid West Africa for the sole purpose of taking slaves to the western hemisphere for this purpose alone. The saddest part is that the idea came from a Pope, who thought they would save the American Indians who were dying under the pressure of European forced labor. Africans were considered hardier and of lesser status. The Western European countries—Britain, France, Holland, Spain, and Portugal—profited from the trade. It can also be claimed that the Industrial Revolution was, in part, funded by the trade. Ports such as Liverpool and Bristol can trace their wealth back to this trading.

Slaveholders and the country at large benefited from this free labor in the north and south of the United States. The South itself became completely reliant on slavery, and it is undisputed that cotton and tobacco farming would hardly have existed without African slaves. Slavery did stop in the northern states for a mixture of moral and economic reasons. However, it continued to function in its most horrible form in the southern and border states. I will not go into detail of the evils of this slavery, as it is only too well documented by worthwhile historians. Those silly stories of the happy slave working for George Washington and Jefferson are myths. It was just that some slaveholders were nicer than others, which can never excuse such an institution. Those slaves who did buy their freedom were never really free, as they could always be identified by their color. In fact, there is no other slave structure in the history of man that was based on race and color.

While the British, French, and Dutch colonies granted freedom to their slaves, the United States continued right through to 1863 and had to fight a war over it. What was even more disgusting was the relationship with Haiti. The slaves of Hispaniola revolted under Toussaint L'Ouveture and fought and won their freedom in 1795, and when Napoleon tried to reimpose slavery, they fought back and won independence in 1804. Yet the United States refused to recognize Haiti because it was African-controlled. The irony of all things was that the Louisiana Purchase was only possible because of the Haitian revolution.

The United States War of Independence was fought with all its glory over the issues of freedom and self rule, but not for the millions of Africans in shackles across the country. That great freedom fighter Patrick Henry issued the phrase "Give me liberty or give me death," then went home and beat his slaves. Thomas Jefferson may have thought about freedom for the slaves, but chickened out when it came to the issue. Independence from King George was obviously correct, but the implementation will be forever tarnished by slavery. The only leader with any credibility was Thomas Paine, and the founding fathers rejected him.

The Civil War was fought over one issue: the right of the Confederate States to continue slavery. Some of those Southern soldiers may have fought bravely, but the cause was wrong. After the war, emancipation, and the Fourteenth Amendment, there was hope that some justice would be granted to African-Americans. We had a Black senator, and Congressmen from the South and in Washington DC. Howard University opened. This was all short-lived, and by the late 1870s the old South reasserted itself, and segregation became the norm. The Klu Klux Klan took over and all African-Americans became second-class citizens and denied every right imaginable. Schools were completely segregated across the southern and border states. After *Brown v. the Board of Education*, one Virginia County just closed all Black schools.

From that time until the civil rights era of the 1950s and 1960s the South remained completely segregated, while the northern Blacks were left in the ghettos, denied many jobs, and mostly ignored. The Klan and its associates continued to harass and attack Black Americans with impunity. The greatest evil of all was public lynching, of which over one hundred cases are acknowledged; numerous others will never be known. There were bright spots during this period, such as the founding of the NAACP and great centers of Black middle-class success in New York, Washington DC, and even Atlanta, Georgia. To understand this period, I recommend reading Gunnar Myrdal's *An American Dilemma* and Ralph Ellison's *The Invisible Man*, as well as John Hope Franklin's *From Slavery to Freedom*. I also challenge any other racial group, ethnic group, or class to show comparable suffering or deprivation.

The one group of Americans who can challenge my claim is, of course, the American Indians or Native Americans. They were here long before any European colonizers' arrival. They are obviously of Asian extraction and controlled the North American continent. It was, in fact, their land, but divided up into different tribes and groups. This land was taken from them, and they were subjected to forced labor. It was not slavery as it was for the Africans, and in some instances, they were treated as equals. Pocahontas was honored as a guest in England, but died from their diseases. Since that time, Native Americans have suffered in the West by the encroaching Europeans, who not only took their tribal lands, but killed them in continuous wars when they resisted. For all of these horrors, I will make the following comparisons: In the twentieth century, many lived on reservations where separate schools existed, but for all other areas no segregated schools, restaurants, or other public facilities were imposed. There was no evidence of public lynching or planned denial of voting rights. The biggest difference between Blacks and American Indians will always be appearance. Within Washington DC and most of the East Coast, the American Indians I have met appeared white and were treated as such. One of my earliest roommates upon arriving in DC was an Amreican Indian who was accepted by the landlady. She resisted any thought of a Black moving in. The best example was the senator from Colorado who claimed Indian ancestry, but looked white except for his ponytail hair style. Even in Hollywood, with all its fighting in westerns, the Indians were treated better than African-Americans. Blacks were always maids and faithful servants. While the Indians could be brave warriors and associates of the white man, most of the "good guys" were kind to the Indians, and the mixed-race offspring were portrayed by Caucasians.

The largest minority in the United States today is, of course, the so-called Hispanics. Such a definition in itself belies any reasonable claim to minority status. Under the current definition, anyone whose language is Spanish or who has a Hispanic name can be classified as Hispanic. This could mean that King Juan Carlos of Spain can come to the United States and be so classified. One of the leading

Republican commentators, Linda Chavez, is classified Hispanic, but does not speak Spanish. In Florida, with its large Cuban population, all Cubans are considered Hispanic. Yet, under Batista, they were pleased to rule Cuba to the detriment of fellow Cubans of African descent. Only after Castro took control did Black Cubans have a role in that society. It is true that the large number of immigrants from Mexico and Central America have been placed in lower-class status in our society. They are often identifiable by their slightly brown skin, but still cannot compare their status to that of a Black person in Alabama during the inception of the United States today. What is more offensive is when a Hispanic who is blue-eyed with blond hair makes claim to special minority status, I will agree that the majority of Hispanic immigrants in this country are similar in economic status to poor African-Americans. However, the origin of this status can be traced to Mexico and Central America, is similar to the peoples of Eastern Europe who came through Ellis Island. It should also be noted that maintaining a separate language does not make for minority status. One thing I have observed is that anti-Black attitudes are as prevalent in the white Hispanic population as in other peoples of European descent.

Asians are also legally classified as minorities and are physically identifiable when compared to persons of European origin. The Chinese came here under forced labor regulations to build the railroads, though not as unpaid slaves. Japanese immigrants were interned during World War II. These events were wrong, but still do not compare to the treatment of slaves or the continuous denial of basic rights to which the large number of African-Americans have been subjected. Once again, I note the comparisons that Hollywood placed on those groups compared to Blacks in the 1930s, 1940s, and 1950s. The superstars could have Oriental girlfriends, and no one ever belittled their mental ability. With Asians, we include the peoples of the Indian subcontinent. The majority are new arrivals who came after the civil rights era and have not been judged for three hundred years by the color of their skin. Modern day USA is in many ways under the domination of Asians in business and science, and we should be proud of their contribution. However, using them statistically to deny opportunity to the people who were to be rewarded under the civil rights laws is unfair.

Arabs are another group that arrived in the United States in great numbers after the civil rights era. They are not classified as minority except for those of African descent. The majority of Arabs are of the Muslim faith, and our society sometimes confuses one with the other. It is apparent that Arabs and Muslims assimilate well with their Black members in mosques and other public places. Whenever I drive by the major mosque of Washington DC there is genuine integration amongst attendees. This cannot make up for the fact that so many Muslim taxi drivers will soon give a vituperative analysis of African-Americans to white passengers such as myself. The store owners who serve the Black public have similar attitudes. What should be clearly understood is that the number of people of African descent in Arab countries is a result of continuous slave raiding into East Africa during the nineteenth and into the twentieth century. This trading was just as vicious as any practiced by Western Europeans in the seventeenth and eighteenth centuries. During

Arabic slavery action, it was only some decent Westerners who opposed the activity. However, it does appear that Africans were assimilated into Arabic and Islamic culture after most slavery ended. There is some evidence that Arabic slavery continued well into the twentieth century.

Islam is a religion of North Africa and countries or areas on the southern edge of the Sahara. In all probability, the majority of slaves who came to the western hemisphere were non-Muslim and, of course, not Christian. It was the habit of slaveholders who imposed their religion on slaves, whether Christian or Muslim. In the seventeenth and eighteenth century, only Ethiopia was Christian and Judaic. Egypt still had a large Christian population, but no slaves in the United States came from there. Is there discrimination against Muslims in this day and age? The answer is yes. It may be unfair, but Americans are suspicious after the events of the last twenty years. We should not judge people by the actions of some, but no one can ever claim that African-Americans ever practiced terror like a few so-called representatives of Islam.

Jews and all members of the Jewish faith have played a prominent role in United States society and have had a direct impact on African-American life. They are identified as a religious group rather than race. After two thousand years of scattering all over the world, there is no certain racial identification. The famous nose can be seen on any Semitic group from the Middle East. The United States has always had a large Jewish population, mostly from Russia, Germany, and other eastern European nations. They have assimilated into United States communities, and some have separated only by their own choice. Many have chosen to anglify their names—a Weinstein becomes a Williams or Smith. Yes, Jews have been discriminated against, but in the United States, no comparisons can be made to the suffering of African-Americans. Some examples: Denial of entry into country clubs and positions in some companies are documented, and there was one lynching in Atlanta. Some attitudes by prejudiced whites were and are often irrational, but in my eyes cannot compare to anti-Black prejudice. Yes, Jews suffered in Russia and, of course, under Hitler, but this did not occur in the United States of America. I will always agree that Jews were the greatest supporters of the civil rights movement compared to any other white or religious group. but as I have noted earlier, even amongst Jews, anti-Black statements have still raised their ugly heads. However, I reiterate my statements made in the biography. I feel more secure entering a room full of Jews than any other ethnic or religious group.

It is very important that I reflect on the contributions, or lack thereof, by the people of the British Isles. They were the main source that started the United States of America and where I came from. They started United States slavery and benefited from it along with all the other European powers involved. The inhabitants of these lands were a mixture of Celts, Anglo Saxons, French, Normans, and Vikings. They developed a language that is a mixture of all and now dominates the world. The majority of slaveholders in the United States came from there, and today most African-Americans have English, Scottish, and Irish names. In the eighteenth and nineteenth centuries, these same lands started the Anti-

Slavery Society, placing pressures upon the United States to change. They can be proud of William Wilberforce and Dr. Livingstone, but also admit to accepting Lancashire mill owners who supported the South to gain cheap cotton based on slavery. Today, people of British origin can be found in the Klu Klux Klan as well as strong NAACP supporters.

People of Irish origin claim a special status in United States society, and someone with an Irish great-grandfather will emphasize that origin, while ignoring other relatives of German or Italian origin. This adherence to Ireland is buoyed by the claims of discrimination against them, as though they have suffered equal to other minorities. It is true that some employers in the nineteenth century did post signs saying "No Irish need apply." This did not stop the New York Police Department from becoming predominantly Irish and denying jobs to Blacks. It does not help the fact that Savannah, Georgia, was 50 percent Irish throughout its history of segregation. Many Irish have been great supporters of African-American rights, and we will always remember the Kennedy family as a political force for good since the 1960s. However, others such as Fox's O'Reilly and Pat Buchanan never fail to appeal to white racism to promote their position. I feel very strongly that many of the claims of anti-Irish bias are religious. British power in London was based on the Church of England with the monarch as its head. They considered anyone Catholic and beholden to the Pope as the enemy. They ruled and controlled the Catholics and other upstart Protestants such as Methodists, who were not part of the Church of England and were classified below par. Some of this thinking was part of the reason for the American Revolution, and we have in the Bill of Rights freedom of religion to stop the domination of the Church of England. Most Irish are of Celtic origin, and so are the Scots, Welsh, and the peoples of Devon and Cornwall. The IRA of Northern Ireland should be called the CRA,{Catholic Republian Army} because they had been oppressed by the people of Scottish descent who were Presbyterian and Celts.

The largest European groups of immigrants in the United States are German. But in the twentieth century, due to their country being classified as the enemy in two world wars, they have become more reserved in identifying themselves. They have made great contributions to the country since their arrival in the nineteenth century. Many fought on both sides of the Civil War and made considerable contributions in post-Civil War industrial development. A large population can be found in Wisconsin, where they brought many socialist ideals. Washington DC had a sizeable German population, making a major influence on its development. However, I am sorry to say, it actively joined in implementing its segregation and upholding it during the twentieth century.

The immigrants who arrived in the late nineteenth and early twentieth centuries were from Italy, Greece, Poland, and other Eastern European countries. They arrived after slavery, but during the height of segregation in the south and witnessed the great migration north of many Blacks mid-century. The majority of these immigrants accepted the status quo concerning African-Americans, believing them to be one class lower. As with all people, some rejected these stereotypes and became great advocates for change. The great congressman from New York, Vito Marcantonio, was a strong supporter of Black civil rights long before the 1960s. My great benefactor Father Gino Baroni was Italian, as is my daughter-in-law. My gravest concern is that for so many years, white Americans of all national origins failed to act to correct the evil of racial segregation.

As an immigrant from England who grew up during World War II, I will always remember the arrival of so many young Americans who fought and died to save us. Their support changed the world and they are often referred to as a "special generation." When I came to Washington in 1961, I met and worked with many ex-GIs from the war. I am sad to say that the majority did not approve of my position on integration. At the present time, many of these men no longer espouse harsh racist views, but do not regret the evils of segregation in World War II and the era right after. We must be proud of all those who fought in that war, but especially those Black Americans who served while being treated as second-class servants.

The United States is the most religious country in the Western World. More people attend Christian services, and the number of denominations is beyond the comprehension of Europeans. The concept of freedom of religion based on the rejection of dominance by the Crown and its Church of England started it. The boost came with the arrival of so many different ethnic groups who, in turn, were persecuted for their beliefs in the old country. In looking at all of the Christian denominations, it appears to me that only the Society of Friends consistently opposed slavery and segregation.

Some of the Methodists and Episcopalians did join forces with Blacks, but segregation created the AME Zion Church and all-Black churches. It was always understood that, for most of the early years of the twentieth century, 11 AM on a Sunday was the country's most segregated hour. The Catholic church was no exception and Washington DC was full of Black and white Catholic Churches. I note that the Catholic school system was only desegregated just before *Brown* v. *The Board of Education*. The church where we were married was St. Paul and Augustine, an amalgam of a white and Black church.

A very important event in U.S. history is also related to this section. The Scopes trial of the '20s brought forth the paranoid opposition to evolution. This was, in part, due to the proof that all humans are related and that people of African descent are equal to Europeans. In this day, opposition to evolution is based on the religious belief that everything stated in the Bible is true. This idea is followed emphatically in the so-called Bible Belt. This region is none other than the old segregationist South.

The Communist revolution in Russia and most parts of the world is now over. Some countries such as China and Cuba still claim that identity, yet it is basically finished, especially in China. African-Americans should always remember that the Communists of the 1930s and '40s were often their only hope. It is probable that the motive of the party was in part opportunism. However, they were one of the few organizations actively trying to overcome segregation across the South.

The segregationists used the anti-communist thinking in the '40s to bolster their cause. McCarthy and his ilk could rely on Southern representatives in Congress for support.

In my opinion, one of the greatest African-Americans in history was Paul Robeson. He was castigated for his attachment to Russia, yet he was given no other choice. This country, along with left-thinking politicians in Europe, gave him the support that he deserved. I can remember the respect and admiration he was given in my Methodist community.

During the Civil Rights movement, in the 1960s, many white churches did show support, but it was the strength of the Black church and its leaders that carried the day. The so-called Bible Belt across the South was a bastion of segregation, and it was from these churches that George Wallace and Jesse Helms got their support. Today, the Jerry Falwells have Black members, but have never asked for forgiveness for past evils.

The two political parties have a lot to answer for in regards to their history in the treatment of African-Americans. After the Civil War, Democrats became the bastion of the South, appealing to those who cherished a return to slavery and the subjugation of all African-Americans. In other areas, it was more the support of all the poor classes as long as they were white. The Franklin Roosevelt administration pursued a more egalitarian program, but the South maintained its segregationist ideals. Southern Democratic senators and congressmen perpetuated segregation and the denial of the vote to Blacks, and stopped every effort to making lynching illegal. The civil rights movement brought about change, and Lyndon Johnson sealed it with the Voting Rights Act. The majority of white voters in the South switched along with their representatives to the Republican party.

The Republican party, thanks to Lincoln and his northern Abolitionist associates, were the saviors of the slaves. Some may question Lincoln's motivation, but we must always glorify his achievements. From that time on the Republican party became the hope and support of African-Americans. It could have done more, but compared to the Democrats, it achieved something. The New Deal changed the picture, and as Republicans promoted more conservative and pro-business ideals, poor Blacks were abandoned. But with the start of the civil rights movement and the election of JFK, the Democratic party became the choice of most Black Americans. It gained votes from African-Americans, but probably lost more when the majority of white men moved to the Republican party. The Republican party exploited this throughout the South and in many areas in the North and Midwest. They used advertisements in their campaigns that indirectly appealed to white racism.

This dates back to the first Goldwater campaign of 1964; Goldwater claimed to be a conservative who believed in state rights. The only issue that mattered to the country, at that time, was the 1964 Civil Rights Act, which would make discrimination against African-Americans illegal. Goldwater opposed the bill and was chosen as the Republican candidate. He was trounced, but carried the Jim Crow states overwhelmingly. I never heard him say that he was ashamed to accept those obviously racist votes. From that time, on, the Republican party has used this appeal to those voters at the expense of the Democrats. Today's Republican party is not considered racist, but an element is still there, such as the senator from Mississippi, and no one can ever forget Katrina.

I have lived most of my life in Washington DC and am proud to be a Washingtonian. From its beginning, race has always been a factor in its development. Under the leadership of George Washington, it became the capital in an area ten miles by ten miles, incorporating two ports of Alexandria and Georgetown. Slavery was in effect there and was part of the new city. Slaves were a valuable commodity to the contractors building the White House and the Capitol. Slave trading was actively pursued until 1850 and only stopped because of the influence of Northern abolitionists. The people of Alexandria became worried about this influence North of the Potomac, and in 1846, before the trade was stopped, had negotiated to take their section out of DC. Since that time, only the area north of the Potomac became Washington DC. During the Civil War, the city became the bastion of the North, surrounded by slave states that fought or supported the Confederacy. In 1862, the slaves of Washington DC were emancipated and, of course, many Blacks soon crossed the DC border to gain freedom. The other little-known factor was that the DC slaveholders were paid to emancipate. Imagine today a drug dealer being convicted, but compensated for stock that was confiscated.

After the Civil War, there was a period of progress for Black Washington. Laws were passed to stop segregation and some voting rights were granted to all citizens. There was a limited council called the House of Delegates. However, by the end of the 1870s they were taken away because of the alleged corruption of Governor Shepherd (appointed). Congress, by then, was coming under control of some Southern Democrats who had already eliminated Black voting rights in the South. Now Congress ruled the city with its district committee and its appointed three commissioners. Basically, Washington became a Southern segregated city until the 1950s. The one bright spot in the city for African-Americans was Howard University. This great institution was started immediately after the Civil War and named after General Howard, who was a leader for the North and supporter of rights for the freed slaves. Around the University area grew LeDroit Park and U Streets, which became a center for the growing Black middle class. Washington, by the 1940s, had a higher percentage of highly educated and successful Black citizens than any city in the country. This does not negate the fact that a larger number of Black citizens lived in abject conditions and were limited to menial jobs.

The Black population of DC was always larger than other northern cities, never less than 28 percent, rising to over 40 percent in 1940, and well over 50 percent in 1950. By 1960, it was a 70-percent Black city. It was these numbers that molded our development and provided the continuing reason for our denial of democracy. Congressmen from across the South, with constituencies containing a larger Black population, were elected based on the denial of rights to African-Americans. They brought this thinking to Washington and used it to promote their popularity back home when election time came. Even their Northern counterparts went along with the status quo. In 1945, there was not one city in the United States that would have considered it acceptable to have a Black mayor. It should be noted that at the original founding of the capital, there was an understanding that it was not a state, but just a center of government. By the Civil War, Washington was not a place where government met occasionally, but a major city, and its citizens deserved democracy like the rest of the nation. When I came to Washington in 1961, we had a larger population than five other states, all of which had two senators and one congressman. Today we have an elected mayor, a city council, and a congresswoman who can't vote. This government can still be vetoed by Congress.

During our short period of semi-home rule, we have been subjected to constant criticism from the outside. Suburbanites and the rest of the nation still refer to us as the murder capital when many other big cities have a much higher rate. They think our government offices are inefficient when they have never used them. No one forgets Mayor Barry and everyone points to him as a reason to criticize our democracy. We cannot tax the commuters who use our services because the suburban Congressmen would veto it. I clearly remember attending a driver safety course in Montgomery County, where the instructor promoted every safety regulation, but repeatedly criticized the rules being applied in DC.

The major newspaper of Washington DC is the *Washington Post*. I have been a daily reader since 1962 and consider it a first-rate purveyor of the news locally, nationally, and worldwide. Prior to the 1950s it had supported the segregationist status quo, but by 1960 had become a strong advocate for civil rights. Its detractors on the right labeled it left-wing or liberal, but in my opinion, it was very middle of the road. The only consistent liberal feature has been its political cartoonists—first Herblock and now Toles. In the 1970s when under attack by Vice President Agnew, it seemed to bend over backwards to mollify the Right in its editorial pages. Today, it still seems to bend over to the right by endorsing certain local Republicans. Its Op Ed page uses writers from the right and moderate left. One writer stands out for writing consistently good articles, of which the *Post* can be proud: Eugene Robinson.

Africa, its history, its geography, and its culture are extremely important to all Americans, especially those of African descent. Yet knowledge is often lacking and many are misinformed. I will note a few concerns: It is one huge continent consisting of multiple countries and tribes, yet many Americans think of it as all the same. The people of Ghana and Mozambique are thousands of miles apart, with completely different cultures and history. If I were to say the Irish and the Greeks are just the same, people would call me stupid. All Africans South of the Sahara are dark-skinned and have been subjected to European colonialism, but this does not make them all alike in culture, religion, and history. I have even heard African-Americans refer to Nelson Mandela as the president of Africa. Some people say all Africans look alike. I challenge anyone to look at a Nigerian and an Ethiopian and say they are the same.

The reader may think that I have no criticism of African-Americans but that is definitely not true. The recent statements of Bill Crosby ring true in many areas. Crime amongst the poor in any society has always been prevalent, but the tendency to glorify it should not be acceptable. The vast majority of African-Americans have suffered through years of denial by society, but through sheer determination proved themselves and become valuable members of society. Their standards should not be marred the actions of a few as our society lumps them all together.

On a personal note, I make the following criticism: When I came to the United States, many Black American men were making their hair processed like whites when they had perfectly attractive heads. Then they became militant and let it grow, saying it was an afro. Today we have a variety of styles, from dreadlocks to weaves, which some still claim are identified with Africa. If you go to Africa, however, the vast majority of men and women have short hair, and the only ones with different styles have copied from Western Blacks. The exceptions are certain tribes in East Africa, which is not the origin of American slaves. As for dreadlocks, they came out of Jamaica by people who worshipped Haile Selassie, who never wore them. The saddest belief of Black males is that light-skinned African-American women are more beautiful. I have heard this pronounced so many times by people I know and admire. Even the BET network will increase the lighting on Black women more than they do their male partners. I will agree that Lena Horne was a beautiful woman and great singer, but not because of the lightness of her skin.

Looking at the United States and Washington DC in my seventieth year, I can say unequivocally that for the average Black American life is much better than 1961. This does not mean all is good for 2007 and anti-Black racism is behind us. Look at Katrina, police shootings in New York, and the poverty rate for those at the bottom of the pile. What we have to realize is how bad things were. This is especially true for the Jim Crow states; today, cities like Atlanta are probably far better than Detroit. The Southern white men accept that change is here, but still vote for the Trent Lotts and their ilk.

David Palmer, at the conclusion of these memories and opinions, makes the following observations and statements: First and foremost, I wish to apologize to any who are offended by my views and statements. I freely admit that generalities are not an indictment of all people in a group, but this does not detract from the fact of what I have seen, heard, or felt. When I started on my plans to come to the United States of America, I thought I knew its history, geography, and culture. Like most Europeans, my concepts were based on basic history, Hollywood, and TV. I even thought the events of Little Rock and Governor Faubus represented an isolated incident, and did not know that African-Americans were 11 percent of the population. Arriving in Baltimore in 1961, still believing in basic Christian principles, I was shocked to discover that the YMCA was segregated. I could only think of my friends from the 1940s, Pat and Olive Robinson, who would have been denied entrance. From that point on, as I was constantly reminded by the attitudes of white Americans that I met, my position on race became one of the most important issues in my life. In those days, there was no reluctance by the majority to express anti-Black views to me, and they thought I understood. It may occur less frequently at this time, but it will still occur, and sometimes in a more subtle form. I believe that my English accent may encourage them. I do not make any claim to great integrity on my part, just what my mother would call stubbornness. There are many who have done far more than me in the struggle for racial equality. I grew up resenting class structure in British society, but this was a piece of cake compared to anything experienced by African-Americans.

I have often been asked why I have developed such strong views on anti-Black racism. I can only conclude that my background, resenting class distinction, was an influence, as was my childhood friendship with a Black brother and sister. However, it was an evolving process, and social status is far less important than the horrors of overt racism and oppression instituted since those first slaves came to our shores. As an individual, I am often guilty of getting carried away with my feelings and being overly critical of people and situations. For instance, when I meet an Englishman with a posh accent, my back is up immediately, even when the person means no harm. The same goes for a white Southern accent and country music that does not mean to offend. As for those who are the recipients and go along with the denial, we can call them Uncle Toms or the equivalent on a class basis. Yet, we all have to survive. As my mother would have said, David is just "stubborn."

LaVergne, TN USA
23 September 2009

158738LV00001B/35/P

9 781604 942583